# RESTORING RESTORERS

## A Vulnerable Treatise
## For Those Who Are Called To Rebuild

Taken From Haggai, Zechariah,
And the Personal Life
Of a Struggling American Pastor

# RESTORING RESTORERS

## A Vulnerable Treatise
## For Those Who Are Called To Rebuild

Taken From Haggai, Zechariah,
And the Personal Life
Of a Struggling American Pastor

Rick C. Howard

**Naioth Sound and Publishing**
Woodside, California

*Restoring Restorers:*
*A Vulnerable Treatise*
*For Those Who Are Called To Rebuild*
Published by:
Naioth Sound and Publishing
2995 Woodside Road, Suite 400
Woodside, California 94062
ISBN 0-9628091-7-9

Editorial Consultant: Cynthia Hansen
P. O. Box 866
Broken Arrow, OK 74013

Cover design: Greg Lane, Inspired Graphics
712 Washington Circle
Hartselle, AL 35640

Text Design: Lisa Simpson, Words Unlimited
1423 W. Toledo
Broken Arrow, OK 74012

Printed in the United States of America.

# FOREWORD

There is no time in human history that Christian leaders have needed to be possessed by God's heart of passion and compassion for the broken more than they do now. Evidence abounds around us that Satan *"...has come down to* [us], *having great wrath, because he knows that he has a short time"* (Rev. 12:12). From the ravaged landscape of New York City to the ripped and ruined soul ransacked by human pain — personally, domestically, physically, economically, spiritually — the need for *restorers* has been amply revealed.

So many Christian media models suggest instant remedies; however, God's Word seldom does. And in the light of that Word, Rick Howard speaks to us *from* the heart of *the* Father and *with* the heart of *a* father. His seasoned and proven ministry invites thoughtful leaders — indeed, *every* sensitive soul — to do three things:

- To be comforted by the message here;
- To be strengthened with patience for his or her own role of service;
- To be confirmed in the promise that *"joy comes in the morning."*

The patience of a "restorer" in the pursuit of effective leadership is a seldom-sought commodity, but it will always be found at the foundation of any truly abiding success. Although this book makes no claim of being a guide to the achievement of success, it fosters the nurturing of those foundational traits that will always be found in those who succeed at the greatest accomplishment of all — to *truly* serve to heal human hurt and to *truly* help people toward hope and recovery.

May you hear God's loving commission to the pursuit of such a mission. May you also be assisted toward succeeding in that mission with the inspiration and practical resources that Rick Howard provides here — transmitted to these paper pages from the "daily-life pages" of a godly shepherd with prophetic insight into our times and pastoral wisdom that is workable in our lives.

In the Name of Jesus,
the Master Restorer,
*Jack W. Hayford*
*Pastor, The Church on the Way*
*Chancellor, The King's College*
*and Seminary*
*Van Nuys, California*

\*\*\*\*\*\*\*\*\*\*\*

My prayer is that every believer would catch the vision detailed in this book. The prophetic acts of praying congregations can and will transform the spiritual atmosphere over our cities. Yet many churches remain wounded and sidelined. Here is a message of hope for all those who dream of seeing their church healed and reenergized.

Rick Howard is a gracious encourager, an effective writer, and a dynamic leader whose teachings always awaken God's people to new dimensions of devotion, praise, and effectiveness. I know Rick's heart — his compassion for people and his passionate desire that everyone see clearly the perfectly loving character of God.

In this book, we discover an in-depth explanation of certain parts of the book of Zechariah alongside the starkly honest confessions of a veteran pastor. It's a combination that draws the reader into a life-changing discovery of truth — particularly truth about the grace of God.

At a personal level, many of us have long possessed a sense of direction and of a possible inheritance from God; yet we continually feel stalled, blocked, and reduced to a mere struggle with survival issues. We know there is more; we suspect a more meaningful, fruitful life is possible. But day follows day, and things remain the same. (Does that describe you?)

There is no greater gift than encouragement with understanding — the kind of God-empowered teaching that lifts us out of old patterns of thought and changes our behavior forever. Today's spiritual leaders — indeed, all of us who call ourselves believers — need the insights in this book. Here are the answers we have cried out for, clearly stated and biblically based.

*John Dawson*
*Founder*
*International Reconciliation Coalition*

# CHAPTER 1

Several of us had ridden the horses out the five-mile trail from the backpacking campsite. It was the third day of a primitive youth camp at which I was speaking, high in the Sierras east of Fresno, California.

My sleeping quarters at the campsite was a family-sized tent, which I shared with Gordon and Elizabeth, a young married couple who had already become a great part of my emerging ministry. The first two nights of the camp had been uneventful. However, camping was not my style, and I felt strained and uncomfortable as I attempted to adjust to the rugged setting.

We finally reached the destination of our long horseback ride, breaking into a clearing where a small ranger-managed station was located. While the others took care of an item of business for the youth camp, I took advantage of the ranger's telephone and called back home to Dublin, California, where I was then pastoring.

My wife Anita's voice sounded wonderful — deep and sexy as usual, but sounding unusually bright this particular morning. "I have bad news for you," she said with a tangible note of irony. "Monday night they elected you to the Redwood City Church!"

I was shocked. Sure, I had met with the leadership and even preached for the congregation. But I had such mixed emotions about this pastorate. I knew the church had been too split to agree on anyone up until then. They'd already gone through the entire selection process without reaching a verdict!

My mind was reeling as Anita continued to talk. I was happy where I was. I pastored a fine young church in an area I knew would soon become a major community of northern California. I had deliberately planned my move there, knowing that it was consistent with a developing young pastoral career.

But Redwood City! Aside from the problems that had surfaced to divide the church, there was also the fact that the congregation largely consisted of another generation — an older group of people I didn't easily identify with. Even their buildings spoke of an era of church development that I found personally unattractive.

"Don't worry," I heard myself saying to Anita. "I don't think that's what God intends for us. It will be all right. I'll see you Friday night." With that, we said our "love yous" and "good-byes."

As I walked away from the outdoor phone, I saw my friend Gordon standing nearby. "Well?" he asked, grinning.

"They elected me," I mumbled. We got on our horses to start back to camp.

"Well," he said again, "what are you going to do?"

I rode silently for a few moments. The scenery was spectacular. There was nothing like the Sierras for a clearing of the mind!

"Oh, don't worry," I said, smiling. "I'll think of something. They don't want an answer until Sunday."

And we both laughed uproariously.

# CHAPTER 2

Y ou can ask anyone who has ever taken on the task of restoration, and you'll get the same answer. Whether the person is in the field of contracting, furniture-building, or counseling, he will tell you that restoration is expensive, time-consuming, and often ultimately disappointing.

The hilarious American movie "The Money Trap" documents one couple's attempt to remodel and restore an aged house. Most people who saw that film laughed on the outside and cried on the inside as they painfully identified with the difficulty of such an adventure.

Why even try to restore? A entire generation of American architects and construction executives simply decided to tear down the old and erect concrete monoliths of hygienic simplicity. Certainly that course of action was a much easier one to take, but the results were less than satisfying.

Today restoration efforts are taking place in the downtown areas of Boston, Massachusetts; Savannah, Georgia; Baltimore, Maryland; and San Francisco, California. All these projects have proven the worthwhile nature of restoration — not just from an aesthetic point of view, but for the profound emotional security that is derived from visiting the wonderfully restored elements of a remembered past. People often find such an experience reassuring, warm, and gratifying.

But then again, this book is not about buildings. The restoration of individuals and of certain church congregations can be even more difficult and disillusioning than the restoration of dilapidated physical structures. That's what I was destined to learn when God placed me in the Redwood City church restoration project more than thirty years ago. Today I write these words largely as a result of what I learned from the heartache and the great blessing of that experience.

In reality, life is meant for restoration. Even the most dire prophetic messages acknowledge that after every judgment imaginable is carried out upon this earth and upon this current age, there will be restoration — not annihilation.

Twenty-five percent of the Old Testament scriptures are either prophetic messages or detailed narratives regarding two calendar events in Israel's history — the eventual Babylonian captivity and the ultimate restoration of God's people from Babylon to Jerusalem. The almost trivial documentation of every detail of these events calls even the most casual Bible student to attention. God must be really interested in this topic — or at least He wants *us* to be interested!

The focus of this book is not so much on principles and details of restoration, although these must ultimately be addressed. I want to center my focus on a more unusual aspect of this biblical material — the restorers themselves.

The writers, often courageous men, were caught up in this inevitable identity with the heart of God. In most instances, they were not "superpeople" charged with supernatural understanding. In fact, many of these God-ordained restorers seemed to be thrust into their destiny with not so much as a manual to guide them and subsequently overwhelmed by the consequences of their involvement.

Restorers often seem to be as much products of their present times as prophets are products of a coming era. Restorers are transitional people who must seek their own encouragement as they fulfill their responsibility of leading others.

That's the reason for this book's title *Restoring Restorers*. This brave, although often frightened, minority is a consequence of God's commitment to history and His almost inexplicable tenacity to the covenant He has made with His people. Those who find God's heart on this matter bear witness to it with their own, almost fanatical devotion to their commitment to continue until the restoration process is completed.

I remember an outstanding female minister who often blessed our congregation in our early days of restoration at the Redwood City church. She had in fact identified with the congregation at one time and was then later released in leadership among us. Her visiting ministry was often humorous but always prophetic and convicting. She made no apology for warning our congregation that she found us dilatory in carrying out prophetic change. On one occasion, she tearfully told the following remarkable story.

"I didn't want to come back here," she said. "There has been so little response, so little change. I believed there were better and more open places for me to spend my time. And so I argued with God when I sensed Him urging me to return."

Her face then became unusually solemn as she continued her story.

"I asked God, 'Why? Why should I go back to those people? They are hard and unchanging.' But suddenly God showed me a man standing in that place." She pointed to the front right of our sanctuary and then continued, "The man had his hands raised and his eyes closed. Tears were flowing freely down his face. I was captured by his intense desire.

"Then I heard a word from God as clear as anything I have ever heard. *'I have a covenant with that man,'* God said."

Later as I pondered this woman's words, I wondered if the man she saw in that vision looked remarkably like me!

# CHAPTER 3

I entered this vale of tears as the fourth child to a shocked forty-seven-year-old father and forty-year-old mother, and three equally surprised older siblings, the youngest of whom was thirteen and the oldest of whom was easily old enough to be my father. It was 1938, which was not such a glorious year for a great entrance or a "coming out."

The place of my birth was Toledo, Ohio, where my father pastored a developing Pentecostal church. I never knew the town personally. Were it not for passport applications and endless landing cards in my subsequent travels, I'd probably not even remember its name.

Shortly after I was born, my family moved to Conneaut, Ohio, where the only childhood pictures in my memory emerge. I remember a tub on a tree stump — my first swimming pool — and "Uncle Dutch," my brother's new father-in-law who often took me to an ice cream store down the street. I also recall the house we lived in — a dark and overwhelming house according to my childish perception.

Conneaut was a city of relatives, although I wasn't conscious of that fact until later. First, there were my father's two brothers and their families. One brother was respectable and upstanding, the other was a town drunk who made the lyrics in the song "Bill Bailey" a reality (his name was even Bill!). Dad's sister also lived in town. She had married Mom's brother, but he had subsequently left her with seven children and an embarrassed church to deal with (in which he had held the position of elder).

Yes, Conneaut was to hold many later memories for me — even romantic memories. But at this stage of my life, it was simply a place of transition for my family. Dad was traveling a lot as the superintendent of a small group of churches.

Meanwhile, Mom had her hands full with three children still at home, including her unexpected "surprise package." Despite the challenges of home life, however, Mom managed everything pretty well. She had the snapping eyes and the equine temper of her Irish Brady upbringing and succeeded in keeping everything lovely and comfortable for her family.

And then there are my memories of the trains! My relatives (including the aforementioned Uncle Bill) had an extensive background on the Nichol-Plate railroad.

Lake Erie also holds many memories for me. Besides being the body of water on which my father once worked as a ferryboat operator, Lake Erie somehow became a mysterious documenter of much of my life.

My memories also include a small Pentecostal church on the railroad tracks (yes, "on the tracks" is actually quite accurate!). The church building must have once been a train depot of some sort. I also have vague memories of more relatives on both sides of the family — some of whom I have yet to place.

During the time we lived in Conneaut, I stayed for a few days with my big brother Bob and his new bride Doris in a rented cottage normally only used for summer traffic. I was just a toddler at the time.

One day after we had returned from spending time down at the lakeside, Doris bathed me and told me to stand by the upright wood stove. As I was standing there getting warm, I dropped my towel and bent over to pick it up. In the process, my posterior hit the front of the stove, and "KALAMAZOO" was branded across my backside in a painful introduction to trademarks.

Bob and Doris were frightened by my subsequent howling and eventually got my absent parents into the act. I now remember the entire incident as a forewarning from God — *"Watch out for hot places and exposed anatomy!"*

I guess I've been clutching the towel pretty hard ever since.

# CHAPTER 4

In an episode of the popular comic strip "Peanuts," Snoopy the dog and Woodstock the little bird are sitting together on top of Snoopy's doghouse.

Snoopy asks, "What are you doing here? You're supposed to be out somewhere sitting on a branch chirping. That's your job. People expect to hear birds chirping when they wake up in the morning."

With that, Woodstock flies off to a nearby branch and belts out a single "Chirp!" Then he flies back to the doghouse.

Snoopy says, "You chirped only once; you can't brighten someone's day with only one chirp."

So Woodstock flies back to the branch and belts out six more chirps. This time when he returns to the doghouse, Snoopy smiles and says, "There now! Didn't that give you a real feeling of satisfaction? The bad news is, you're supposed to do that every morning for the rest of your life!"

Snoopy's "bad news" is simply more than Woodstock can handle. He drops over in a dead faint on top of the doghouse.

Do you ever feel the way Woodstock did as he lay on that dog-house contemplating his lifetime duties of chirping? I certainly do. I wonder how I ended up where I am, doing what I am expected to do.

You see, I'm a restorer, plain and simple. I drool over old, forgotten buildings and dream of their potential beauty. Many of my friends favor tearing down the structure and building anew. *After all,* they reason, *it's cleaner, more modern, and definitely safer.*

Of course, the concept of restoration has a much deeper significance than as it pertains to Georgian architecture or "art nouveau." Restoration often has to do with societies, families, churches, and specific relationships.

My contention is that restoration is deep in the heart of God. He delights in honoring ancient covenants when even those who initially made those contracts with Him seem to have forgotten them. The Word solemnly declares that ours is a God who keeps covenant:

> "Therefore know that the Lord your God, He is God, the faithful God who keeps covenant and mercy for a thousand generations with those who love Him and keep His commandments."
>
> Deuteronomy 7:9

Clear patterns concerning restoration emerge in the Bible, none of which is more dramatic than the restoration of crucial elements of Jewish life after seventy long years of Babylonian captivity. As I mentioned earlier, Bible scholars have estimated that twenty-five percent of Old Testament scriptures deal with that specific captivity, including the prophetic warnings of the coming judgment, descriptions of actual events that occurred during that period, and prophecies of a future restoration. I have dealt with this area of teaching in much of my teachings and writings, as I know *many* teachers have done in countless ways.

The discussions in this book, however, center on two major views of the restoration, found in the books of Haggai and Zechariah. My purpose is to identify clear patterns for restorers today and to include some extremely candid illustrations from my own personal experiences. Again, my focus is on the restorers themselves — those who were absolutely committed to the goal of beginning again, often at the expense of their own reputations or personal safety.

True restorers are often in need of restoration themselves, especially in the midst of seemingly impossible projects in which they feel firmly entrenched. Thus, we come to our subject of *restoring restorers*. Does God really care about the restorers themselves? Isn't He primarily interested in the same thing most people are — the pragmatic victory of completion, regardless of how the goal is achieved?

I believe the answer to that last question is *no*. God *does* care very much about the individuals who commit themselves to restoration in their own lives or in the lives of others.

When Israel's captivity ended, a call went out for restoration from an unexpected source — King Cyrus of the newly emerging body of the Medo-Persian empire. Ezra reports that the Lord stirred up Cyrus' spirit to make a proclamation throughout all his kingdom, which included the absorbed former Babylonian empire that had conquered the Jews in 786 BC (Ezra 1:2-4).

The "stirred-up" group of Jews who responded returned to the blackened circle of earth that was the judged and forsaken Jerusalem. Ezra details Cyrus' instructions, the release of the finer temple possessions from the Persian treasury, the names of those who returned to Jerusalem, and how they went about doing it. It's worth your careful perusal.

## What Did the Rebuilding
## Of the Temple in Jerusalem Represent?

The returning Jews had a clear restoration priority — *to rebuild the formerly glorious temple in Jerusalem*. With true heroism and noble, unselfish enthusiasm, they began rebuilding the house of God.

These restorers saw the temple as the center point of a restored nation, for it had always been central to the national life of Israel. Even during the Israelites' years in the wilderness, the tabernacle was located in the dead center of the twelve tribes, and every tent of every tribe was given its reference according to that central tabernacle.

Thus, the rebuilding of the temple was more than just an act of dedication and faith for these returning refugees; it was a grand symbol of the continuity of the present with the past, a reminder that God's purpose and Presence still remained with His people. For these reasons, the returnees postponed many considerations of personal convenience as they began to rebuild the temple of God.

In every arena of life, these kinds of God-chosen tasks will arise on occasion. They often have to do with reclaiming a fallen standard, reliving a purposeful dream, or rebuilding a broken but God-anointed project. It is to such moments and such works that God calls His restorers. His honor is at stake; His choice is obvious. He will restore the restorers, and they will do their part in fulfilling His purposes.

So whether in our home and family, our church and society, or the excruciatingly personal arena of our own lives — here's to restoration, the joy of beginning again!

# CHAPTER 5

B ack at the youth camp, I awoke in the middle of the night feeling restless. My friends, Gordon and Elizabeth, were sleeping soundly in the other corner of the tent.

What was I feeling? It wasn't just a nagging need to urinate — such a constant inconvenience on a cold, Sierra night. It was something else — nausea, and even more, *pain*.

I got up and stumbled out of the tent to the latrine. Maybe it was my imagination, and it would all go away when I relieved myself.

Gordon was always a light sleeper, as well as being uniquely sensitive to me. I heard him come into the temporary "place."

"Are you all right?" he asked.

"I don't think so. But then, who knows?" I joked feebly.

Then the pain hit, sharp and nauseating. I doubled up and began to experience dry heaves.

"Hey, that doesn't look good. Where do you hurt?"

"Can I tell you where I feel good? I think that would be easier," I groaned.

"I'll get someone," he said, and I stumbled back into the tent.

Elizabeth was now awake as well. It's hard to sleep when folks are having fun, and my night of agony was in full swing!

"It's probably appendicitis," the rotund camp director diagnosed. "We'd better get in touch with the rangers."

The rest of the evening was a muddle of sights and sounds for me. Someone drove the jeep over the horse trail, bumping through brooks and over rocks. Someone else held me like a baby doubled over in pain in the front seat, and Gordon straddled the back.

Everyone around me prayed prayers and gave me loads of compassion, but I simply wanted to die. The pain was awful enough without the "joy ride," but the combination of the two was devastating.

Hours later, we reached the clearing. An ambulance awaited us, and medics offered me some relief as they rushed me to the hospital. I gritted my teeth and gripped anything I could grab as the ambulance raced toward its destination.

Gordon was riding along with me in the ambulance. "Do you think this has anything to do with Redwood City?" I asked him as I lay there, grimacing in pain.

"Beats me," Gordon answered.

I remember saying, "Oh, God, I hope not!" before surrendering to the gray cloud of medication.

# CHAPTER 6

I read a paragraph in a recent work of nonfiction that greatly enlightened me. It seemed somehow irrelevant to the overall theme of the actual book, yet it provided me with a bit of amazing advice.

The central character, a man named Jim Williams, is asked how he intends to reverse a disastrous series of personal calamities in his life. He responds, "The same way I restore houses: step by step."

Jim then quotes a college professor who once told him that an old house would defeat you if you tried to restore it all at once — roof, windows, weatherboarding, central heating, wiring, etc.

"You must think of doing one thing at a time," he indicated. "First you say to yourself: 'Today I am going to think about leveling off the sills.' And you get the sills leveled. Then you turn your mind to the weatherboarding, and gradually you do all the weatherboarding. Then you consider the windows. Just one window at a time. That window right there. You ask yourself, 'What's wrong with that *part* of that window?' You must do it in sections, because that's the way it was built. And then suddenly you find the whole thing completed. Otherwise, it will defeat you."[1]

Restoration by its nature always looks impossible. What's more, it seems highly unlikely that the finished project will even be worthwhile. "Who cares?" and "So what?" seem to be obvious and understandable reactions.

Restoration demands a longer, more painstaking process and is often more expensive. That's why the question is more often "Is it worth it?" than "Can it be done?" How many will say that something bright, shiny, and new wouldn't be better?

That must have been the quandary facing the first refugees to return to Jerusalem and the temple ruins after the Babylonian captivity. Jerusalem had been left a blackened piece of earth by the most thorough and complete sacking in history under Nebuchadnezzar. One must always remember, however, that the actual judgment against Israel was from God Himself and that the prophet Jeremiah had predicted a seventy-year captivity for the sins and omissions of God's people (Jer. 25:11,12).

It is significant that young Daniel, who was taken in one of the earliest waves of that judgment, years before the final destruction, acted as a "bookend" for the entire captivity. It was Daniel who, near the end of the seventy years, wrote this:

> **In the first year of his reign I Daniel understood by books the number of the years, whereof the word of the Lord came to Jeremiah the prophet, that he would accomplish seventy years in the desolations of Jerusalem.**
>
> **Daniel 9:2 *KJV***

Perhaps Daniel began to count on his fingers the way I sometimes do. As he did, he remembered how long it had been since he had been taken into captivity. "It has already been 68 years!" he

---

[1] John Berendt, *Midnight in the Garden of Good and Evil* (New York: Random House, 1994), p. 299.

might have said. "The time of the prophecy is about to be fulfilled." Upon that realization, Daniel took upon himself the responsibility to confess his people's sin to God and to intercede for them so the prophecy could be fulfilled.

Through Daniel's years of captivity, he served in the highest capacities within the courts of foreign rulers. Serving first under three Babylonian kings — Nebuchadnezzar, Belshazzar, and Darius — Daniel ultimately served under Cyrus himself during the transfer of power from the Babylonian to the Medo-Persian empire.

Perhaps Daniel actually showed Cyrus his own name in biblical prophecy — a message recorded four hundred years before Cyrus' birth (Isa. 44:28). However it occurred, Cyrus accepted his biblical role. Ezra, who most carefully documented the restoration of God's temple, recorded the event this way:

> Now in the first year of Cyrus king of Persia, that the word of the Lord by the mouth of Jeremiah might be fulfilled, the Lord stirred up the spirit of Cyrus king of Persia, so that he made a proclamation throughout all his kingdom, and also put it in writing, saying,
>
> Thus says Cyrus king of Persia: All the kingdoms of the earth the Lord God of heaven has given me. And He has commanded me to build Him a house at Jerusalem which is in Judah.
>
> Ezra 1:1,2

Now, the thought of the Lord God of Heaven stirring a heathen king to do what had once been undone by divine purpose must have been a shock to the ears of any Israelite. It would be like Saddam Hussein announcing he was a closet Charismatic! But what followed added insult to injury.

> Who is among you of all His people? May his God be with him, and let him go up to Jerusalem which is in Judah, and build the house of the Lord God of Israel (He is God), which is in Jerusalem.
>
> Ezra 1:3

Had God given the trumpet call for restoration through the mouth of a Gentile sovereign? How could that be?

The year of Cyrus' decree was 536 BC. What follows this highly unusual proclamation occupies the biblical record of Ezra, Nehemiah, Haggai, and Zechariah. This single decree proved to be a secular "stone" that would start an avalanche of history. Ultimately, it would result not only in restoration, but in the continuation of the biblical prophetic purpose that would culminate in the coming of the Messiah — Jesus Christ.

The events that followed this decree are a chapter in prophetic history that deserves a study in itself. The roles of Ezra and Nehemiah are especially fascinating to focus on as they deal with the many difficulties that arise in the midst of restoration.

Approximately 50,000 Jews either volunteered or were chosen for this first wave of restorers. It is generally agreed that these people did *not* represent "the cream of the crop."

You see, most of the Jewish people had become well established in the business and economic life of their captive nations. Therefore, those who were willing to go were largely people without great hope in their current circumstances, such as those without inheritance and the elderly. It reminds one of the first description of the malcontents and the "down-and-outers" who would ultimately become David's mighty men: *"And every one that was in distress, and every one that was in debt, and every one that was discontented, gathered themselves unto him..."* (1 Sam. 22:2 *KJV*).

*We must all learn to lead the available in the instant of the immediate.* Jesus fed the multitude with the most meager of resources. In every arena of life, this is a principle of beginning. Restoration almost always begins with those who may never accomplish its ultimate purpose.

Leaders and priests for this first wave of counter-captivity probably had to be conscripted, as were those who comprised the latter wave of returnees under Ezra.[2] However, in whatever manner these people arrived and for whatever reason they came, Ezra provided a faithful biblical accounting of each of their names. Such attention to genealogy hadn't been given since the earliest stages of Israel's beginnings. God obviously cares about those who help rebuild!

In the Old Testament restoration, two men were selected to lead: Zerubbabel, a direct descendant of King David; and Joshua, a descendant of the last high priest and ultimately a descendant of Aaron himself.

God always puts a name on restoration. Whether occurring on a national level, a local level, or even within a family, restoration is ultimately personalized. Therefore, the temple to be built would be known as Zerubbabel's temple, or the Restoration temple. Although it would be greatly expanded and beautified under King Herod, it would be Zerubbabel's temple in which the Messiah would manifest Himself.

It was an exciting moment when the first 50,000 returnees arrived in their native homeland. How could they have imagined that they would ever have a role in such a divine purpose as this?

The United States is missing this kind of tragedy in her background. We are perhaps the only nation in the world that has not known the national tragedy of being conquered by an outside nation.

Talk to folk from Poland, Hungary, Germany, or Russia, and they will tell you what captivity and war is like — what it is like to see your home burned, your crops destroyed, and your children murdered before your eyes. They'll tell you what it is like to leave all your money and half your family behind in a divided nation as you run to a totally foreign nation to learn a new language and start life over again at fifty or sixty years of age.

---

[2] Read carefully Ezra 7.

This was the background of this unlikely group of restorers traveling to Jerusalem. How happy (albeit still somewhat confused) they must have been when they began rebuilding the temple under Zerubbabel and Joshua!

The minute the people began to rebuild the temple, however, opposition arose. As always, the opposition came in two parts. First, there was external opposition from the people of that country who didn't want the Jews to rebuild the temple. A rebuilt temple stood for something these people didn't want — a renewed nation.

That is exactly Satan's attitude toward the Church today. He cares nothing about the human energy of the Church. He is unmoved when we organize ladies' groups, men's groups, children's programs, Sunday schools, choirs, usher teams, and so forth. We can do that until Jesus comes, and the enemy will leave us alone. But when we get on our knees to "rebuild the temple" — when we begin to stand for God's values within secular culture — the opposition of both Satan and worldly society becomes adamant.

If you are familiar with this particular story of restoration in the book of Ezra, you will remember two characters named Sanballat and Tobiah who led the opposition. This opposition group was made up of mixed Jews — folks who had stayed after the captivity and intermarried with neighboring people and who weren't about to see a standard of holiness raised again in the land.

However, let us admit that internal opposition also existed. Zerubbabel and Joshua did their best to see that the temple was rebuilt. Yet some of the old men who had come with them out of captivity stood around crying because the restored temple wouldn't be as great as the former grandeur of Solomon's temple.

As a result of the opposition of both of these groups, the work stopped. For sixteen long years, it was only a good idea lying dormant. The call of God to build was stopped, and the people sat around feeling sorry for themselves.

What ultimately happened to these early Jewish restorers is a lesson for all who would attempt to rebuild. When opposition arose, they stopped their grand cause — the rebuilding of the temple — and turned their attention to the personal and the secular. Each person began to build his own house, to do his own thing — and, in the process, each gave up his role in the restoration to which God had called him. The eternal purpose was surrendered to the mundane, private concerns of the individual.

For their disobedience, the people reaped dire consequences. A serious economic depression ensued, complete with crop failures, droughts, and even more opposition. All the returnees' rosy dreams seemed burned up in smoke. Indeed, the people of God were in a desperate moment of their history.

Suddenly God stirred the spirit of a prophet named Haggai, himself an aged man who should have been in prophet's retirement. Haggai shook off the limitations of his age and went forth to declare for God that the people needed to get on with the job of rebuilding the temple.

Haggai was a blunt hammerer, neither philosophical nor diplomatic in the way he preached. He simply preached to the people to get them motivated to obey God.

Perhaps Haggai's greatest victory was to bring a young priest out of the shadows, a friend of the prophet named Zechariah. When Zechariah saw that this aged prophet was willing to be the brunt of the people's animosity in order to get them started, the young priest stood up and said, "I'm going to take my stand too."

Zechariah means "the Lord remembers" or "the one whom Jehovah remembered." This in itself is very interesting, for there are no coincidences in God. The young man who was to take on the preeminent task of getting the Israelites to return once again to their task of rebuilding the temple was a man whose very name means "Jehovah hasn't forgotten us" or "Jehovah remembers His people."

Perhaps we should also underline the fact that Zechariah first had to identify with God before he would receive revelation from Him about the task ahead.

Too often our own reaction to the Word of God is calloused. We can sit through two and a half hours of watching a mechanical shark push its way through the ocean to terrify a seacoast city, and we never miss a beat. But the thought of spending twenty minutes in the Word of God is too much. Nevertheless, we tell the Lord we want more revelation. "Why don't You speak to me more, Lord?" we ask.

Christians are often just as confused as the world. "What should we do under these circumstances?" they ask. "Where should we invest our money? Should we build? Should we move? Should we stay? Should we do this? Should we do that?"

I look at this type of Christian and think to myself, *Is God dead? Doesn't God speak anymore? After all, it's the Word that says, "Wherefore be ye not unwise, but understanding what the will of the Lord is."*[3] *Is that Word no longer real and vital to these people?*

However, eventually the Word does come to those who care enough to listen. This principle is so clear in the first chapter of Zechariah.

You see, God doesn't reveal Himself to folk who aren't on the right side to begin with. Zechariah first had to declare himself. He had to stir himself up, awaken out of spiritual slumber, and say, "I'm going to stand up with Haggai. He's right. We must quit building our own houses and get on with the work of God."

Only after Zechariah took this stand did he receive his first word from God:

---

[3]Ephesians 5:17 *(KJV)*

> Be ye not as your fathers, unto whom the former prophets have cried, saying, Thus saith the Lord of hosts; Turn ye now from your evil ways, and from your evil doings: but they did not hear, nor hearken unto me, saith the Lord.
>
> Zechariah 1:4 *KJV*

However, hearing from God wasn't an overnight process for Zechariah. He had to wait three long months before God gave him any specific revelation.

At this point, Zechariah does an amazing thing in this call to repentance. He asks, "Where are your fathers now?" In other words, Zechariah is saying, "Where are the prophets now who spoke their words from the Lord? They're all gone." Then Zechariah goes on to say in the next verse, "The Word overtook your fathers, and God has done exactly what He purposed in His heart to do. We spent seventy years in captivity, just as He said" (Zech. 1:5,6).

This is one of the most interesting words in the Scriptures. When I see a congregation of people, I can close my eyes and remember thousands of congregations just like it to whom I've preached during my many years of ministry. Yet I've never been to a church where someone doesn't say, "Yes, Grandma So-and-so used to sit over there. Brother and Sister So-and-so used to sit there. So-and-so used to pray at this altar. But now they're gone."

So it is with ministers and prophets. Great men of God have come and gone at the desk of every church.

It was my privilege within the first five years of my rebuilding at Redwood City to bring back all the former pastors to minister to our church. All of them had been involved in laying the foundations of the work. For this they were to be honored as wise master builders who had been used of God in the ministry.

In the pulpit of our Redwood City church, great prophets have also ministered to us: Leonard Ravenhill, Corrie ten Boom, Campbell McAlpine, John and Joy Dawson, as well as many others. Some are now dead. Many other voices have ministered over the years in revivals and other special meetings, all of them preaching for the Lord, many of them now gone.

Zechariah asked, "Where have your fathers gone? Where have the prophets gone? What is the only thing that lasts? Answer: *the Word of God*!"

The Word of God has continued throughout the ages. It is always the touchstone by which the true nature of all else is measured. In fact, Zechariah said, "The Word followed your people, your fathers, like a missile until it overtook them."[4]

Believe me, I understand the evangelical quandary. I understand that most of us just slip away from our busy, workaday business world once a week to worship God for a few hours. I understand that building houses, raising families, working at our jobs, and making investments can easily become our only reality. But the truth is, we will one day go the way of all flesh and join our fathers in the grave. One day our lives on this earth will be over.

The prophets who are raised up by God must also go the way of the flesh, but the Word of God is eternal. What a person does in reference to that Word is the only thing that ultimately matters. The most important thing any of us will do this week is decide how we will react to the eternal Word. That daily decision is destined to overtake us in our day.

Only when Zechariah took his stand on the Word did God say, "I've heard you, Buddy. I'm going to test you for three months, and then I'm going to reveal new revelation to you."

I believe that's true in any church and any place. God will not reveal Himself to the carnal and worldly-minded. He cannot reveal Himself to Christians who spend five times the amount of time in front of a television set as they do in His Word. God will reveal

---

[4]Paraphrased from Zechariah 1:3-6.

Himself to those who have made a priority commitment to His Word.

Look at what happened when Zechariah took *his* stand! One January night in Shebat, God gave him eight visions! (You know, of course, that visions are *not* dreams. When you have a vision, your eyes are wide open; you *see* events happening. Thus, you cannot say that it is merely a fantasy that occurs in your mind.)

In a few hours' time, revelation exploded in Zechariah's heart as God took him from the beginning to the end of Bible prophecy. Zechariah was to be a prophet as well as a priest! Probably no prophet in the Bible received such panoramic revelation as Zechariah did that night. It's simply incredible!

As a result, Zechariah would ultimately prophesy of the Messiah riding on a donkey's colt. He would see the future Israelites asking the returning Messiah, "Where did You receive these wounds in Your hands?" Zechariah would hear the Messiah answer that He had received them in the house of His friends. The young prophet would also see a millennial kingdom with "Holiness unto the Lord" written on the pots and pans. What a phenomenal thing happened to Zechariah when he took his stand on the Word of God!

That January night was a night of history! God would let Zechariah sleep for a while; then He would wake him up. If you read the first six chapters in succession, you'll see that Zechariah would have one vision and fall off to sleep. Then the angel of the Lord would come and wake him up again to show him something else. In this way, Zechariah was able to receive an incredible amount of revelation from God in the space of one night.

Think about the quote that began this chapter about restoring an old house: "...You ask yourself, 'What's wrong with that *part* of that window?' You must do it in sections, because that's the way it was built. And then suddenly you find the whole thing completed. Otherwise, *it will defeat you.*"

Restorers are a very human lot. They have an unusual belief and see a difficult vision. However, their calling and purpose is lived out in very real ways.

Zechariah is ultimately raised up with a prophetic word to refresh a group of discouraged restorers. He finds the key in identity with God's heart and His Word. But Zechariah's direction is the *people* who, although discouraged, are yet imperative in the task of restoring a fallen purpose of God.

I believe the early words of Zechariah are a pattern for us. We, too, are often discouraged in the task of restoration set before us. We often make the mistake of trying to quickly restore everything at once. We easily become dismayed when vital, opposing voices misinterpret our purposes.

Frequently in Zechariah are the words, "I lifted up my eyes and saw…" That is always the task of the Moment. God wants us to *see*.

God wants *you* to see!

# Chapter 7

The doctors at the Fresno clinic medicated me and sent me to the hospital nearest to my home in Dublin, which was Eden Hospital in Castro Valley. "It isn't appendicitis after all," they said. "It looks like kidney stones." I had never heard of such a thing. "Must have been the horseback riding," the doctors added.

*Absurd!* I thought.

I lay in my room, waiting for the coming of a bright new day. There were liquids, magazines, visits, and occasional sympathy. Then my friend, John Alfonso, came to visit me in the hospital. A board member of the church I pastored in Dublin, he had a worried look on his face that I knew had nothing to do with kidney stones.

"Can we talk about this?" he asked sheepishly, and I knew he meant Redwood City. John and I had stood together in the up-and-down days of the infant Dublin church. We often went together into the little church office to count Sunday's income to see whether or not there was enough in the offering to pay the church bills.

John and his wife had provided a sense of family and security to our family during the challenges of those early days. Together we had launched a new Christian school and added an educational unit, miraculously provided through used government "portables."

Now the prospects of Valley Christian Center were finally beginning to look up. The congregation was maturing. John and I had searched out larger properties; we had a clear vision for the future of the church. We'd been through so much together. I could read the hurt and fear in his face as he thought about the possibility of my leaving.

"Do you know about the vote?" I asked, and he shook his head. But he already knew something was brewing. After all, three of the young families in our congregation had been raised in the Redwood City church. They had immediately recognized the board members from Redwood City on their first visit to Valley Christian Center one Sunday morning.

"What were they doing here?" one of the young women had asked me. "I know those guys, and I don't like what I'm thinking!"

How could I explain this situation to my friend? I felt responsible and somehow like a betrayer.

"John, I thought this was all just God's open door for me to share with those people about some things they need to change in their church. I mean, I was *brutal* with that board! I never thought they'd invite me to preach. When they did, I preached on 'Reconciliation' in the morning and 'The Judgment Seat of Christ' at night. Those are hardly 'try-out' sermons!"

John laughed slightly. He knew both of those sermons as well as he knew me.

"It's almost like I've been used, John," I said. "I took each step thinking that would be the last one. Now here I lie, and it looks like kidney stones are calling me to Redwood City."

We both laughed. "Kidney Stones" almost sounded like the name of a Christian rock group! But John knew me all too well.

"Is that what you're really thinking? I mean, has this experience had that effect?" Tears welled up in his eyes, and I found myself getting choked up as well.

"Well, let me put it this way. God sure has a way of getting my attention. I've had a lot of time to think, and I sense that a sovereign order of God is surrounding this move."

He nodded, his head bowed, and someone else came in. I was somewhat glad for the interruption; I've never been very good at those kind of moments. When the physical crisis passed the next day and the nurse triumphantly showed me the "little fellar" on a gauze patch, I couldn't believe so little a cause could generate so much sound and fury.

But a wind was blowing. Jesus had given a clue when He said, *"The wind blows where it wishes, and you hear the sound of it, but cannot tell where it comes from and where it goes. So is everyone who is born of the Spirit"* (John 3:8).

I was being blown across the Bay. I could feel it, and I was still holding on to the bed.

"Hi, friend." Gordon had just arrived and stood at the door of my room. "All better now?"

"Yep — I even have the bullet," I joked.

"Looks like Redwood City, huh?"

"Either that, or a horseback ride in the wrong direction," I answered.

He knew exactly what I meant.

# CHAPTER 8

W hat had been the word that stirred young Zechariah to identify himself personally with the need for restoration? It was a simple yet powerful word, designed to break the bonds that had kept God's "first cause" for the returnees unfinished for sixteen years. This word came from an aged prophet, numbered among the returnees — one old enough to have seen the original temple before the seventy years of captivity had even begun. His name was Haggai, a word that means "festive" or "festival," implying "the festivals of Jehovah." This probably means that Haggai had himself been born during one of Israel's festivals, which were always times of national celebration and rejoicing.

Can we connect a word from God to joy? We may as well begin by admitting that few of us think a corrective word from God has its foundation or its purpose in joy. Haggai's first word of the Lord was directed specifically to Joshua and Zerubbabel, disturbing the complacency that had allowed sixteen years to pass without finishing a God-initiated project.

Let me ask you a question: Is there anything more important in life than a word of the Lord that comes personally to you? Now, to some people, that evokes images of an angel coming down from

Heaven or a screen dropping from a supernatural cloud that allows them to read a message from God. But you know better than that! God speaks clearly through His words, through His ministry, and often through your own personal circumstances.

For most of us, God's word to us is not as obvious as having a prophet stand and declare, "This is God's word to Rick Howard." Yet still, we can hear the word within our hearts when it comes and know that God is speaking to us.

Do you know the word "tsunami"? It means a huge wave that is generally created in the ocean depths by significant earth movement. In 1989, when a major earthquake occurred in California, it was predicted that a thirty-foot tsunami would hit the West coast as a result of that earthquake. By God's mercy, it never happened; nevertheless, it was predicted.

The first prophetic word of Haggai was an appeal to thinking — an observation from God that was as jarring to the people who heard it as a tsunami is to the coastland it hits. The effect of the message was a great challenge:

> Thus speaketh the Lord of hosts, saying, This people say, The time is not come, the time that the Lord's house should be built.
>
> Then came the word of the Lord by Haggai the prophet, saying,
>
> Is it time for you, O ye, to dwell in your cieled houses, and this house lie waste?
>
> Haggai 1:2-4 *KJV*

Anytime a preacher quotes Haggai, everyone thinks it must be connected with a building program or project. The truth is, however, that God's word always comes to us to do something specific. When it does, we had better hear what God is saying to us and do His will with a firm heart.

My primary reason for studying Haggai has been much broader than the study of an actual building. To me, the real question is this: "What did the rebuilding of the temple in Jerusalem really represent?"

First, let's observe what it does *not* represent. No prophet had given a direct command to anyone about building the original temple. In fact, when David wanted to prepare for the building of the temple, Nathan merely said, *"...Do all that is in your heart, for God is with you"* (1 Chron. 17:2 *NAS*) Nathan may have felt that the tent of the tabernacle was more what God wanted than a temple.

Neither did Haggai's word from the Lord have anything to do with a sacrificial system. We learn from Psalm 5 that, by the eighth century BC (the century in which these prophets lived), God's people were already beginning to understand that the forgiveness of sins was connected with something other than a sacrificial system.

But if not so that the system of animal sacrifice could be perpetuated, why *did* God want the temple rebuilt? First, an entire complex of ideas had grown up around Mt. Zion, a place where God's Name was distinguished. To rebuild the destroyed temple was to let the world know that God was in business! It had to do with covenant. It had to do with blessing.

As mentioned before, the house of God was always central to the national life of Israel. Thus, the rebuilding of the temple for these Jews was a symbol of God's covenant-keeping faithfulness toward them as a people.

Perhaps we must also see from the New Testament that Jesus spoke of His own body as the temple. The Bible says that, when Jesus was raised from the dead, He became the cornerstone of the holy temple made up of living stones. Those living stones were believers who would become the dwelling place of God in the Spirit.

We find those words both in Ephesians 2 and in First Peter 2. We the Church will one day be presented to Christ as the ultimate issue of honor for Him. Therefore, the purpose for rebuilding this physical temple also had to do with God's honor. It was to be a witness and a statement to the world that gave glory and honor to His Name.

May I be very personal and specific on this point? Many Bible scholars consider Haggai to be more of a historical prophet than a theological one. Yet I believe that, in reality, he is one of the most theological prophets of the Bible. No voice in the Bible appears to better address the correct motivation of the human spirit. The consistent emphasis in Haggai is on *priorities*. That's especially true in this first prophecy and message.

Priorities refer to *that which takes precedence in order*. In other words, what should your preference be when ordering the many claims that are made on your time, attention, energy, and material resources?

Please let me be clear. You have a family. You have a home. You have a job. You have children to raise. You have future expenses to plan for and present bills that must be paid. The issue is never whether or not you should be negligent with these basic responsibilities. The issue is always this: *What takes precedence? What are your first priorities?*

For instance, true tithers write God's check first — not after the other bills are paid, but first! Then they trust God and their own discipline to pay the rest of their bills.

Let me quote R. K. Harrison on this:

> Haggai saw God as a holy, righteous and moral Being Who demanded from His people complete obedience in spiritual loyalty. If they manifested His moral and ethical characteristics, they would be true witnesses to His power and they would be rewarded with peace and prosperity while other nations were in the grip of turmoil. Seeking the kingdom in the truest sense would ensure them that all the other necessities would be added to them, whereas a prime emphasis upon material possessions would result in individual and community deterioration."[5]

---

[5]Roland K. Harrison, "Haggai." *Zondervan Pastoral Encyclopedia of the Bible*, 5 vols., edited by M. C. Tenney (Grand Rapids, Michigan: Zondervan, 1975), p. 14.

The words of the people are poignant: "It is not time to build the temple of God." Notice that there was no argument in their minds about whether or not the temple needed to be built. I think I understand what they were saying.

Believe me, if you had stopped and asked these Jews, they would have immediately said, "Of course, the temple of God is going to be rebuilt. That priority needs to be reestablished, but just not yet. Not now! This is the wrong time."

You see, there was eminent confusion in the world during those years. Cyrus had died, and the Medo-Persian empire was in disintegration. It had passed through three other rulers within just a matter of years. The nation that had once been a stable organizer of civilization during that particular time in history had suddenly come apart like a broken vessel.

Haggai knew the determination of these people. They were neither irreligious, unconcerned, nor disinterested. They knew the temple of God should be built. But God was saying to them, "You say it isn't time to do this. What you're really saying is that it is time to build your cieled houses" (v. 4).

That word "cieled" actually describes a kind of cedar ceiling that had originally been used only in the king's palace. Thus, the people had exercised this sixteen-year-long opportunity to build for themselves homes that were stately, almost like the former homes of the kings. But God's question to them was this: "Was this the time for you to be doing that?"

How about you? Is this the time for you to focus on buying new clothes or to put a new emphasis on this hobby or that pursuit?

Hear me — God is concerned about you. He is not a bully trying to take all the fun out of your life. But what is your first priority? Answer that question; then everything else will follow in due course.

God wants to bless each of us beyond what we could imagine. But we must learn to trust *His* order of priorities. This first appeal from Haggai addresses this principle and deals with the challenge of reality — the negative results that misplaced choices have caused.

After Haggai makes an appeal to thinking, he is used of God to address the heart. Here is a call to *consideration*:

> Now therefore, thus says the Lord of hosts: "Consider your ways!
>
> "You have sown much, and bring in little; you eat, but do not have enough; you drink, but you are not filled with drink; you clothe yourselves, but no one is warm; and he who earns wages, earns wages to put into a bag with holes."
>
> Haggai 1:5,6

A false balance in life leads to disaster. God calls His people to acknowledge this.

There are probably five pictures given in verse 6. The first is that of a lean harvest. Without a fruitful harvest one year, the farmer cannot put away the seed that guarantees the harvest for the next year. "You sow much," Haggai says. "You're hard workers, but you're not gaining from your labor."

The second picture is that of a person suffering from a disease. He eats great quantities, but the metabolism of his body will not let him digest the food.

The third picture is even more interesting. It is quite literal in the original language: "You are drinking a lot in an effort to get drunk, but you cannot get drunk from what you are drinking." These people can find no escape in their old, familiar forms of escape. The old ways of forgetting don't work any longer.

The fourth picture is of clothes that don't really protect or provide warmth for those who wear them. Since warmth often speaks of human acceptance, this might be a significant picture of rejection.

The last illustration is of economic distress. The income never meets the needs. Now I just want to say very quickly to you that this is not God's plan, nor has it ever been God's plan. A Christian is meant to enjoy satisfaction and fulfillment in this life. His food, whether little or much, is intended to provide for his needs.

God means for every believer to be able to provide for his needs by his income. That's why this picture He gives the prophet is so significant. These people are seeing very poor results from all their hard work. It is as if they are putting their money in a bag full of holes!

Perhaps you feel like that at this moment. Maybe you've said at times, "I just don't know where all the money goes!" God's response to you may be the same message He gave through Haggai when He said to those called to be restorers, "Your money is leaking out the holes in the bottom of your life!"

Having spoken to the *mind* and the *heart*, Haggai's prophecies next appeal to the *will*:

> "Go up to the mountains and bring wood and build the temple, that I may take pleasure in it and be glorified," says the Lord.
>
> Haggai 1:8

Then God repeats what He has already said:

> "You looked for much, but indeed it came to little; and when you brought it home, I blew it away. Why?" says the Lord of hosts. "Because of My house that is in ruins, while every one of you runs to his own house.
>
> "Therefore the heavens above you withhold the dew, and the earth withholds its fruit.
>
> "For I called for a drought on the land and the mountains, on the grain and the new wine and the oil, on whatever the ground brings forth, on men and livestock, and on all the labor of your hands."
>
> Haggai 1:9-11

Here is a command, of course, for the people to put first things first — to make the rebuilding of God's house the first claim on their time, strength, and resources. "Get on with the job," God is saying. "Accumulate the resources and the energy for the test."

Verse 8 gives the reason for the command: "I will take pleasure in it and be glorified."

I once ministered in England to a pastors' conference in a place called Ashburnham. It is one of the first five estates built in the English empire, going back to the days of the Normans. In its heyday, it was an enormous estate with landscaped yards, beautiful lakes, and barns that look like castles. But one by one, the Ashburnhams all died until, finally, the only living relative was a distant great-grandson studying in a theological seminary. When the estate passed to this man, requiring huge taxes, he decided to give the estate for the purpose of Christ.

God gave the man a promise out of the book of Haggai that the latter glory would be greater than the former glory and that, in this place of beauty, God would give peace. I tell you, when you walk those grounds today, it is easy to sense God's peace.

One of the huge buildings on the estate, a former servants' quarters, has now been turned into a house of prayer where people are praying around the clock every day and night. From all over the world, Christians gather to pray in this world prayer center. When you walk over these marvelously maintained grounds with its flowers and carefully trimmed hedges, you feel the greater glory of the Ashburnham estate.

It is for our sakes that God will not prosper a scheme we devise in order to avoid His Word. We will look for much and gain little. And that which we do bring home, God will blow on it and cause it to disappear. In our hearts we understand this, for the reason is obvious.

"I will tell you why I did this," God said. "When My house was in ruins, you ran to your own house and left it desolate."

# CHAPTER 9

The spring and summer of 1952 was incredible. Sharon, Pennsylvania, had often been an oasis of Republican politics in a sea of Democratic voters. But the political climate was changing. Truman was running again, but a head of steam was building for the military hero, General Dwight David Eisenhower.

What did I know? Well, although I was just a kid, conservative politics was a big part of my upbringing. Republicanism and Chevrolets were "shibboleths" at the Howard house. Besides, for some reason I had been reading about "Ike" for several years and had written school reports on his career and life.

So I started a "Junior Republican Club" to encourage teenagers who were too young to join "Young Republicans" to help with the campaign to elect Eisenhower for President. I figured that we could at least canvas neighborhoods, baby-sit for campaign volunteers, and call people on the telephone. Strangely enough, my idea worked. I recruited all the girls I knew from school and even a couple guys, and the Junior Republican Club was off and running! Soon the *Sharon Herald*, the city's newspaper, picked up the story with the headline "14-Year-Old Boy Registers 81 People for the Coming Election."

Personally, I loved arguing politics and religion, and this seemed like an opportunity to do both. From my perspective, it was a clear case of the good guys versus the bad guys. So I printed blotters to hand out with the words "BLOT Out Corruption and HIGH TAXES" and did all I could to make sure our miniature campaign stayed in high gear all the way to election day.

During this time, I attended Republican Conventions, rallies, and various meetings with the candidates. I was launching what I thought was a successful start to a lifetime political career.

James H. Duff, then U.S. Senator from Pennsylvania, promised me a page-boy appointment, and the *Sharon Herald* again carried my story — "Local Boy Makes Good!" My friends even gave me a farewell party at the end of the school year.

However, around midsummer, an embarrassed Senate staff member called me to apologize. He told me that the senator didn't have an appointment that year, and he had run out of associates to trade with.

I was crushed. *How could this happen?* I asked myself. *What will I tell my friends?* There would be no Washington, no presidentially-signed diploma, no head start for law school and politics.

Of course, boys don't cry. Nevertheless, I couldn't talk that night and went straight to my room. This was no time to pretend to be the strong, macho Marlboro Man. I needed to be alone.

"Son, may I come in?" Dad asked at the door of my room. "I know you're disappointed; but I want to talk with you."

"Can it wait?" I blurted out. I didn't want a lecture, and Dad and I definitely had different ideas about my future.

"Sure. I just have an idea, and I thought it might give you something to think about."

"Oh, come on in," I said dejectedly as I sat on the edge of my bed.

"Son, do you remember our trip to Emmanuel College and Academy last year?" Dad asked. "You seemed to like it there in Royston, Georgia. We've even talked of your eventually going there."

"Sure, sure, I remember. What does that have to do with now?" I asked.

"Well, Mom and I thought you might like to go there next year, since you were already prepared to leave for Washington D. C. This may be a good time for a year away in school."

Now the truth was, I had *never* been as excited about that church school as Dad thought I was. I also knew my family couldn't afford that kind of private education. But, on the other hand, this was really a great idea. An escape plan developed in my mind. I'd go away for the year; meanwhile, everyone would forget the "Local Boy Makes Good as a Senate Page" stuff.

"Yeah, that might be a great idea," I responded. Then I asked incredulously, "But, Dad, how would you be able to swing that?"

"We'll try to find a way," Dad replied. "I just wanted you to have something else to think about." Then he left my room.

I paced for a few moments. *This is a great idea! Living 1,500 miles away from Sharon is a way to avoid all the embarrassing questions!*

But somewhere in the back regions of my mind, a suspicion haunted me. Did God have anything to do with this? We had an understanding, He and I, and this seemed an awful lot like "dirty pool."

*Oh well,* I thought. *One way or another, it's time to get on with life — even if it's in Royston, Georgia.*

# CHAPTER 10

I t's always time to get on with God's purpose — whenever and wherever His call goes forth!

Haggai's prophetic word began to break the sixteen-year stretch of disobedience concerning a God-designed project of restoration. It was spoken by an aged prophet — one of a very few who even remembered Solomon's temple that now lay in ruins.

What courage Haggai manifested! His message was a rebuke of the people's postponement of God's priorities, as well as a rebuke of their chosen lifestyle.

So what happened? Did this blazing prophetic interruption accomplish its purpose? Let us quickly look at Haggai 1:12-15. Although it may seem like we are jumping ahead a bit, the sequence is important for the study of one particular point.

Then Zerubbabel the son of Shealtiel, and Joshua the son of Jehozadak, the high priest, with all the remnant of the people, obeyed the voice of the Lord their God, and the words of Haggai the prophet, as the Lord their God had sent him; and the people feared the presence of the Lord.

> Then Haggai, the Lord's messenger, spoke the Lord's message to the people, saying, "I am with you, says the Lord."
>
> So the Lord stirred up the spirit of Zerubbabel the son of Shealtiel, governor of Judah, and the spirit of Joshua the son of Jehozadak, the high priest, and the spirit of all the remnant of the people; and they came and worked on the house of the Lord of hosts, their God,
>
> on the twenty-fourth day of the sixth month, in the second year of King Darius.

Here's a description of true revival. This passage shows us the clear implications of Haggai's first message. But it also speaks to us about the means by which God stirs up a spirit of restoration. I believe it has personal applications to many of us.

Haggai's message produced holy reverence and radical response as these discouraged restorers gave God their first instance of any true obedience. They heard His words and were stirred. A sense of awe and fear in the Presence of God arose within them.

Notice that God didn't even wait until they actively began to build again. Just on the basis of their reverence for His Presence, God's word came firing back at them like a fiery arrow: *"...I am with you, says the Lord"* (Haggai 1:13).

This is an all-containing assurance that goes beyond any particular age or circumstance. God was saying to the restorers that He would help them and protect them so the rebuilding of the temple could come to completion.

However, the restoration of the temple was only one fruit produced by this divine promise. This word speaks of the Presence of the One who knows all our needs and possesses infinite power to support and to save us. As David said in Psalm 23:4 (*KJV*), *"Yea, though I walk through the valley of the shadow of death, I will fear no evil: for thou art with me...."*

Let me ask you something. Can you say that you know Jesus Christ as your Lord and Savior without also saying with me that the greatest thing in your life is the knowledge that the Lord is with you? This isn't just God's general promise to be with you always, even to the ends of the earth. It is His specific promise to be with you in what you're doing every moment of your life. God says to you, "I am with you in your lifestyle — in every aspect of your daily routine — because you have chosen to obey Me."

Is this God's message to us? Can all of us claim this message as God's promise to us personally? Can we take the unspeakable comfort of these words as we read them right now?

To answer these questions in the affirmative, we must first realize that every promise of God is conditional. We have no right to appropriate this divine promise for ourselves unless we have determined to live in the fear of the Lord and in obedience to God's word to us. Only then does He say to us, "I am with you to see that what I've begun in you is finished."

## Five Issues From Haggai's First Word of the Lord

It's important to review the various issues Haggai's first message addressed as it applies to us today. At least five issues can be found in this message that should challenge every one of us — particularly if we want to join God in His mission of restoration.

### PRIORITIES

Haggai first called on these Old Testament restorers to evaluate themselves by asking, *What time is it?* In modern-day language, he was asking these buffeted believers, "What are you doing that will remain after a test of priorities?"

Haggai also challenges us in this extreme appeal to *put first things first.* The words that begin the Bible should be the words that govern our lives: *"In the beginning God..."* (Gen. 1:1). We cannot complete God's purpose by putting second things first and first things second. When we do that, we put God in a position where He cannot grant us prosperity lest we count His prosperity an excuse for our wrong choices.

Wouldn't it be wonderful if every Christian home and every Christian place of business had a plaque permanently hung on the wall that said, "In the Beginning God"? God is first. He is where everything starts. Every project, every checkbook deposit, every month should start with the understanding that *God is the beginning*.

Jesus said, *"...Do not worry about your life, what you will eat or what you will drink; nor about your body, what you will put on..."* (Matt. 6:25). Then He went on to say more about this first principle of priorities:

> For after all these things the Gentiles seek. For your heavenly Father knows that you need all these things.
>
> But seek first the kingdom of God and His righteousness, and all these things shall be added to you.
>
> Therefore do not worry about tomorrow, for tomorrow will worry about its own things. Sufficient for the day is its own trouble.
>
> Matthew 6:32-34

Let me share with you a paraphrase of those words out of *The Message Bible* by Dr. Eugene Peterson:

> What I'm trying to do here is to get you to relax, to not be so preoccupied with *getting*, so you can respond to God's *giving*. People who don't know God and the way he works fuss over these things, but you know both God and how he works. Steep your life in God-reality, God-initiative, God-provisions. Don't worry about missing out. You'll find all your everyday human concerns will be met.
>
> Give your entire attention to what God is doing right now, and don't get worked up about what may or may not happen tomorrow. God will help you deal with whatever hard things come up when the time comes.[6]

---

[6]Eugene H. Peterson, *The Message: The New Testament in Contemporary Language* (NavPress: Colorado Springs, CO, 1994), p. 24.

I understand from experience the truth of this passage of Scripture. For instance, once when I was ministering in England, I received a call from my local church informing me that an important promised sale of excess church property had fallen through. This sale was extremely strategic to the future plans of our church; nevertheless, a mantle of God's peace seemed to immediately cover the news when it came.

I cannot describe to you the peace I felt; yet with that peace came also a sense of imminent danger for those who opposed God's purpose by preventing the sale of that church property from taking place. But I felt the Holy Spirit's Presence and never lost an hour's sleep from that point on.

That sense of supernatural peace covers every situation you face when you are seeking first God's Kingdom in all that you do. But perhaps you are thinking, *It isn't time to change. There's still time to focus my attention on other interests besides the things of God.* Be careful — the prophet is warning you that if you continue to keep your priorities out of order, the hand of God will have to be against you. You belong to Him; therefore, He cannot promote disobedience in your life. For your sake, He will not bless you until you have "ordered your way aright" (Ps. 50:23 *NAS*), making Him your beginning in all things.

## PURPOSE

Second, Haggai is reminding us that our *lifestyle* declares *purpose*.

I believe that God wants His people to live at the level they are permitted to live as His covenant children. But well-ordered priorities are what establishes His blessing. For instance, a believer's willingness to give sacrificially allows God to abundantly bless him so he can give even more.

Your manner of lifestyle is extremely relevant to your Christian walk. Remember, your primary task as a New Testament believer is not to build a temple of wood and stone. Paul's word to the Ephesians describes the nature of your divine call:

> Now, therefore, you are no longer strangers and foreigners, but fellow citizens with the saints and members of the household of God,
>
> having been built on the foundation of the apostles and prophets, Jesus Christ Himself being the chief cornerstone.
>
> Ephesians 2:19,20

Our number-one priority in life is to fulfill the purpose of God. It's high time that we acknowledge that!

Haggai's call for the people to go up to the mountain and obtain stones for the rebuilding of the temple is a reminder to us that, even in difficulty, danger, or discouragement, we can offer ourselves as living stones to the Lord by which He can build in us a living temple. May we allow God to redirect our priorities so that our lifestyles speak of a higher and greater purpose!

## SELF- EXAMINATION

Haggai further reminds us that there is such a thing as *healthy self-analysis.* He exhorts us to consider our ways. We are to review our history; study our checkbook; take stock of what has happened in our lives in the past year; and evaluate how our conduct has lined up with God's priorities for our lives — the priority of His house and of His people.

Many of the people I pastor live faithfully by these divine priorities. In fact, I often feel embarrassed at the sacrificial response of the people I pastor in times of particular need. At such times, I feel unworthy to lead such a people. Many of them go without, sacrificing material gain that would make their personal lives easier or more pleasurable, in order to further a specific purpose that God has placed on their hearts. However, please realize that just as Haggai's message to the people had to be personally understood by each individual listener, so this word must be personally understood by you.

## THE BOTTOM LINE

The fourth point is obvious. Every true Christian must have only one bottom line: that the Lord may take pleasure in him or her and be glorified. This principle was set forth when God said through Haggai, *"Go up to the mountains and bring wood and build the temple, THAT I MAY TAKE PLEASURE IN IT AND BE GLORIFIED..."* (Haggai 1:8).

You see, if believers don't faint, the harvest will not be little. Some will reap sixtyfold, and others a hundredfold. They will neither hunger nor thirst any longer. He who has mercy on them will lead them into living fountains of water, for God does not rob His people.

God is not in the poverty business, my friend. He is not begrudging you the prosperity you desire. In fact, He will pour out upon your life more blessings than you are able to contain as your heart stays faithful to this word of the Lord spoken through Haggai.

As you read these words, you may be able to say to me without batting an eye, "Those two things express my heart. I want God to take pleasure in me, and I want more than anything else for God to be glorified in my life."

The One who is all-sufficient has no desire to *take from* us; He desires only to *give to* us. However, God only satisfies the soul with bread that comes from Heaven. When we eat this bread, we are filled with true spiritual blessing.

## REPENTANCE

Certainly it is God's love and concern for our true value that causes Him to bring us to repentance. The true reading of the Hebrew clearly implies this in the latter recapitulation of Haggai's prophecy. Concerning the restorers' current circumstances, the Lord says through Haggai that it is for their sakes drought has come in place of rain. God tells the people, *"You looked for much, but indeed it came to little; and when you brought it home, I blew it away..."* (Haggai 1:9).

That doesn't fit well with many people's understanding of a good father. Their idea is that a father should lavishly and without any respect to obedience just give and give and give. But God, who understands fathering better than any person reading this book, knows it is more imperative to build obedience and self-discipline into the lives of His people than it is to grant them immediate prosperity.

These restorers couldn't even escape from their problems by getting drunk. They were putting their money into bags with holes. And even when they did bring home increase from their labor, God would blow it all away!

Oh, how remorseful is this cry: "You have sown much, yet you bring in little." God loves us so much. Not one of us has He ever called by His Spirit yet failed to give a purpose. He will not allow us to be less than that for which we have been created.

When the true tsunami comes to end this present age, God won't be using Hollywood technicians to design disaster. At that time, so many of the things that seem important now will be gone. In a split second, houses filled with possessions will be reduced to nothing.

But those of us under God's mandate are preparing ourselves to be ready for that moment. We know that, even if we were to lose all our possessions on this earth, we have laid aside for ourselves treasures in Heaven where moth and rust cannot corrupt and where thieves cannot break through and steal. That's where the true value lies. God loves us that much.

When we simply reverence God's Word and allow a sense of awe to come into our lives concerning His Presence and His purpose, we can then expect this: God will not even wait for the results before

He says, "I am with you. I'm with you in this now." Indeed, His purpose in restoration will be fulfilled!

Let me ask you at the close of this short review of an ancient prophet's word: Does the Holy Spirit speak to you through His Word? Is it possible that this word of the Lord through Haggai is directed to you as well? Does God speak about priority issues in your life? Is there a genuine sense of repentance in your heart over forgotten issues?

Forget the disobedience of those around you. When God's Holy Spirit brings to you a cry for repentance regarding a specific, identifiable issue in your life, that is then the word of God to *you*. As surely as this word stirred up Zerubbabel, Joshua, Zechariah, and the remnant of God's people, His word will cause a "stirred-up" spirit in you.

# CHAPTER 11

How can I describe my first eighteen months in the downward-spiraling mess that was the Redwood City church, ultimately to be named Peninsula Christian Center?

When we first arrived, the church board introduced us to a Christian realtor who was also a member of the church. We were happy when this realtor found us a nice house — until suddenly the board decided they couldn't help us purchase our home as they had promised earlier. This new development left us feeling embarrassed and the realtor feeling angry. However, I could tell there was more in the shaking of his head than disappointment. As the events of the past months had unfolded at his church, he had looked on with chagrin from his favored place of distance.

It had indeed been a year for these people. After experiencing the loving oversight of a fatherly pastor for fifteen years, the people had grown restless. When this pastor resigned, they searched for a "superstar" minister to turn their relatively normal church into a great Charismatic center. They even entered negotiations to purchase a huge theater complex next to a freeway. Their dreams were big, and they needed a man with the leadership skills to match those dreams.

A pulpit search had located a notable Midwestern pastor with a large, growing ministry, including a radio outreach and a well-known identity as a Charismatic leader. However, the six months that followed his assumption of the pastorate had been disastrous. Something was seriously wrong. The move had left the minister displaced and stumbling. His messages seemed strangely apologetic and repetitive.

People who had remained loyal to the church even as they had grown increasingly restless began to be more outwardly critical. They knew their church normally endeavored to keep ministers for long-term pastorates. But these people believed that, in the case of their new pastor, this practice would be disastrous.

More than one hundred church members left between Sunday school and church on one Sunday. A neighboring church that was The Christian phenomenon on the San Francisco peninsula was for all the marbles to shift every so often. For this church, the shift was definitely in the process of going the wrong way!

The board became wary. Rumors that the new pastor had a moral problem were floating over from his former staff members, and things were looking serious. Two board members had jobs that provided them with investigative resources and experience, so they decided to use their know-how to find out if there was any truth to the rumors. After damning facts started to surface, the board confronted the new pastor, who resigned rather than have the information made public.

Later, with support from other church members, the new pastor tried a stiff-armed "coup d'état" against the board, but they held steady. Another group left the church in support of the pastor, but still the board refused to reveal specifics to anyone when asked.

Charges and countercharges abounded within the congregation and among various members of the denominational leadership. The church board became isolated and defensive, with a measure of self-righteousness mixed in as well. After all, this was war. Meanwhile, church members such as my realtor friend wandered about hurt, generally feeling deprived of information and unresponded to. Subsequent pastoral searches had only deepened the rift and the misunderstanding between the board and the rest of the congregation.

That was the situation I had encountered one weeknight in the board conference room of the Redwood City church. That was the board I was to deal with. They, too, were hurt from being criticized and mocked by hurt, angry parishioners and self-appointed rectifiers of injustice. Some board members were confused and uncertain themselves; yet all of them desired above everything else to be faithful in this time of crisis.

It was an old story. There weren't many clear-cut rights or wrongs in this situation. Instead, there were broken dreams, altered expectations, and a deep, spiritual disappointment as people struggled to grasp the most difficult truth of all — the humanity and failure of God-anointed leadership. What once seemed impossible was happening. Foundations were crumbling. A firmly established church, almost a half century old, seemed to be fragmenting and sliding into the morass of oblivion almost overnight.

And then — dum, ta dum! — into the center of the storm stepped Rick Howard, alias "Super Minister," with his well-polished sword (never used, of course) and a cape of spotless white (or so he thought!).

But somewhere between my receiving the congregational vote and the next board meeting, the board members had begun to doubt me. That explained their retreat on helping my wife and me purchase a home. I was as unprepared for this conflict as a high school boy who is thrown into frontline war combat without any basic training!

# CHAPTER 12

It is not the ultimate purpose of this book to teach from Zechariah or Haggai in a scholarly manner. Yet we must never take scripture out of its context. It is important that we lay the groundwork of what the Word is saying and under what circumstances.

Our principle story concerns Israel in the 520s BC. The young prophet Zechariah was given eight specific pictures on one January night. The Holy Spirit has burned these visions into my soul as being incredibly applicable to the restoration of those who are called to the task of rebuilding and restoration even today.

Zechariah's first vision after he has been stirred by Haggai to become a restorer was a very interesting one.

> Upon the four and twentieth day of the eleventh month, which is the month Sebat, in the second year of Darius, came the word of the Lord unto Zechariah, the son of Berechiah, the son of Iddo the prophet, saying,
>
> I saw by night, and behold a man riding upon a red horse, and he stood among the myrtle trees that were in the bottom; and behind him were there red horses, speckled, and white.

Then said I, O my lord, what are these? And the angel that talked with me said unto me, I will shew thee what these be.

And the man that stood among the myrtle trees answered and said, These are they whom the Lord hath sent to walk to and fro through the earth.

And they answered the angel of the Lord that stood among the myrtle trees, and said, We have walked to and fro through the earth, and, behold, all the earth sitteth still, and is at rest.

Zechariah 1:7-11 *KJV*

Now, there's an intriguing vision! And what's more, it's in Technicolor! Even the horses have colors, although the original Hebrew text is not all that clear about colors. The word for "red" might as easily be translated "sorrow" or "brown" in the Hebrew.

The colors of the horses are probably not significant. What *is* significant is who rides a red horse and where his place is in the vision. The rider is among the myrtle trees "in the bottom" — in other words, in the very lowest part of a valley.

Certainly there must be no question about the implication of this first vision! First, a myrtle tree is a very sensitive, unstately, and easily broken shrub. It is not really tree-like at all! For example, how different it is from the stately cedars of Lebanon to which God had often compared His people. At this time, the people were not stately cedars of Lebanon but low myrtle bushes, sensitive and easily broken. And where were these myrtle bushes growing? In the very low bottom area of a valley. We might even call this area a swamp!

What do you think was being said to Zechariah in this vision? God's people were at their lowest ebb, as low as you could possibly imagine. The temple had been destroyed; Jerusalem was in ruins; and the people of Israel had been in captivity for seventy years. Only a small handful had returned with the money Cyrus had sent to begin rebuilding the temple. But they soon became discouraged and gave up on the work to concentrate on building their own houses. What a low, discouraging, despairing moment of history this was.

But the significant truth God showed Zechariah in this vision was that the Lord of hosts — the angel of the Lord who appeared in this vision — is with His people even in their despair. The "man" on the red horse was the same angel of the Lord who came to Abraham on the plains of Mamre, the same captain of the Lord's hosts who appeared to Joshua before the battle of Jericho, the personification of the Lord Jesus Christ Himself. And where was this captain of the Lord's hosts? He was among the myrtle trees in the low, depressed bottom land or swamp.

Zechariah suddenly had a new perspective of God. God had allowed His people to be judged because their sin demanded judgment as much as if they had been a heathen people. But the God who demanded their judgment was walking among them in the moment of their lowest ebb. This was an incredible truth for Zechariah to grasp!

We who have been raised in strong biblical traditions so often view God as coming to and going from our lives based on our performance. We think, *He's with me when I'm good; He's gone when I'm bad. He loves me when I do well; He doesn't love me when I do badly.*

Of course, that is the exact opposite of the essence of God's revelation. When He has chosen a people and purposed to be with that people, He is with them in the rock bottom or the lowest ebb of their existence as much as He is with them on the mountaintop of their greatest experiences. He is standing in the midst of the myrtle trees, in the low bottom land of His people's experience.

The second truth we must recognize through Zechariah's first vision is that God's angels are patrolling the earth, representing His sovereignty. God is in charge; He is in command. These angels are coming back to the Father and saying, "We have gone to and fro throughout the earth, and all things are at peace. But we have a question, Lord: How long are You going to wait before You restore Jerusalem? How long are You going to let Your people be trampled under captivity?" (Zech. 1:12). Indeed, God is in control.

The book of Zechariah, as well as the books of Ezekiel and Daniel, are imperative books to read and understand if you wish to understand the revelation of Jesus Christ at the end of the Bible. Many of the images God gives Zechariah are later echoed in the book of Revelation. Another significant similarity is that the book of the Revelation of Jesus Christ was written in the same kind of time period and under similar circumstances as the book of Zechariah.

At the time the apostle John wrote the book of Revelation, the Roman Empire had just broken out in its most ferocious persecution of the Christian church to date. It was the time of Nero when Christians were being thrown to lions or dipped in oil and burned alive upon stakes to light the gardens of Rome at night. Seven million Christians would die in those first three centuries of the Church — so many that not enough limestone caves could be found to bury the dead! Even John, the only living apostle who had not been martyred, had himself been poisoned and burned in oil. John must have been one tough preacher to have survived his persecutions — and it was to him that God gave the final revelation!

I remember very well a young man, an avid surfer, who was converted in a southern California church where I served as youth pastor. This young man asked me where to begin in his walk with God. I said, "Go home and start reading the Bible."

He came in to me about three days later and said, "I don't know if it's right to do this or not, but as I was reading the Bible, I went to the last chapter to find out how it turns out. Guess what?" he exclaimed happily. "We win!"

When God revealed Himself to John, He called Himself by the name of *Pantokrator*, which is the Greek word meaning *almighty* or *sovereign*. It is almost purely an Old Testament description.

So how did God reveal Himself to the apostle John during a time when the Church was undergoing one of its greatest persecutions? He said, "I'm the God who is in charge; I am in control; I'm sovereign; I'm Almighty." This was also His way of revealing Himself to Zechariah.

There may be times when we, too, find ourselves wondering, *What has happened to God? Where is He when things seem to be completely out of control?* But God must say to us, "I am *Pantokrator* — almighty and sovereign. My horses still ride across the earth, patrolling it. I am still in charge, and I'm going to bring everything to pass according to the purpose of My Word."

## These Horns Are Meant for Beating

The second interesting vision that God gave Zechariah was of four horns, like the horns of an animal. Zechariah also saw four craftsmen, workmen, or carpenters. These four simple men were not angels or superspiritual beings, but in the vision each of them beat down those horns until they were destroyed (Zech. 1:18-21).

Now, the word "horn" in the Bible almost always refers to *power* or *authority*. Zechariah was standing in a God-forsaken little country with a broken-down temple. He was living in a day when *the* power of the world was the Medo-Persian Empire. In fact, during his lifetime Zechariah had already lived through the reign of two great world kingdoms — the Babylonian and the Medo-Persian empires.

But in this vision, God revealed to Zechariah in his spirit that two more world powers would arise in the future and have the same kind of effect on Israel that the first two empires had. They would also scatter Israel and trample the land God had given to His people. Of course, from our viewpoint looking back, we know those two nations were Greece and Rome.

So God said, "Here are four horns, Zechariah — four powers or authorities." This is what the world always wants to know: "Where's the real power? The United States, Russia, and China are the great powers of the world. That's where the attention must always be."

But God didn't stop there. His message continued: "You must see something else, Zechariah. You must see ordinary men beating down those horns until they are scattered and broken. You must learn where the ultimate power of this world lies."

Do you know how tiny the land of Israel is? Its average width is sixty miles across. At its widest place, Israel is only 120 miles across. In biblical times, Israel was only 180 miles long at its greatest length. You could fit all of this tiny, insignificant land bridge within the state of Massachusetts!

Yet God chose that little country. Think of the powers that existed around it. Think of how the Egyptians must have laughed at it with their chariots, their power, and their gold. Think of how each power that followed — the Babylonians, the Medo-Persians, the Greeks, and the Romans — must have joined in the derision.

Yet Israel exists today! The modern-day world has no Egyptian, Babylonian, Medo-Persian, or Roman empire, but it does have the nation of Israel. Israel's ability to survive is truly one of the incredible stories of history and demonstrates that true power is not found in the measure of man's might.

Let's talk about us who are Christians for a moment. Our tragedy is that too often we are not single-focused. We say in our hearts, *I believe in the Word. I believe in the purposes of God.* But at the same time, many of us are also attracted to the world's idea of power.

For instance, we might think, *Wouldn't it be something if I had a suite of offices in a leading high-rise with nineteen secretaries and twelve telephones on my desk! I could pick up a phone and call the New York Stock Exchange direct and say, "Sell ten thousand shares of AT&T," and the entire market would crumble at my words!*

Other Christians' fantasy is to be in Washington D. C., sitting at a desk with a direct line to the President, knowing that he has a hot line to China or Russia. Bombarded on all sides by the world's way of thinking, these believers have come to believe that this kind of "inner-circle" position is where real power lies.

It is tragic that some of us really believe this in our inner man. But God must respond, "How foolish you are."

These powers — whether kingdoms, civilizations, economic systems, or the United Nations — may rise like great horns, but ultimately they are beaten into the dust by common workmen, common craftsmen, common carpenters.

In England there once lived a simple housewife named Susannah Wesley. During her entire lifetime, she never ventured more than sixty miles from her home, but she did a superb job of raising ten children.[7]

Susannah did a great deal of laundry and baked a lot of pies, I'm sure. More importantly, she faithfully gathered her little children about her and taught them the things of God.

How ridiculous it would have seemed to the lords of Parliament in that day had you said to the Parliament chairman, "You men may be the decision-makers for this nation, but you are *not* where the action is! The real action is with a little housewife in the middle of England who is raising ten children, two of which are going to arise and change the direction of English history!"

The historian Lecky, who is not a Christian writer, wrote often of the fact that John Wesley single-handedly changed the course and direction of English political life. He further claimed that the ministry of John Wesley was the primary reason the bloody French Revolution did not eventually envelope England. A great catastrophe was averted — all because of one man with the Word of God!

---

[7]Susannah Wesley actually gave birth to nineteen children, but only ten grew to adulthood. She home-schooled her children during their elementary years. The boys in the family were so well-prepared by their mother's instruction that they were able to go to Oxford University at the age of sixteen with only one year of preparatory school.

We must not live in a dichotomy. If we do, there can be no revelation for us, nor will we experience any movement with God. We cannot say, "The action is with God," but inwardly hold the commitment, *If only I could have this or be in this position, then life would be different. That's where the power and authority is.*

God says, "Forget it. Horns will rise, but ultimately they will be beaten to the earth. Your purpose must be in line with My Word. That is where true power lies."

# CHAPTER 13

Where do you go to find out about the Medo-Persian empire today? Well, you might dig in the dirt in the right place. But even then you'll find little — perhaps a few shards of broken pottery.

This is what the great Medo-Persian empire has been reduced to. Today the way we trace this ancient empire is primarily by archaeological study. So it is with the Roman empire, and so with many other world powers of days gone by.

Perhaps the hardest lesson for Zechariah to learn was to see the world greats of his time, such as the Medo-Persian empire, the way God saw them. Zechariah had to stop thinking that all real power rested with King Darius!

And how about us? Do we think real power resides at the United Nations? If we are to be spiritually encouraged and strengthened, we must set our eyes on the eternally sovereign God, realizing that His Word will be the breaking point of all eternity.

## Tit for Tat

Zechariah's third vision was of a man with a measuring line. This was a picture of God preparing to return and rebuild the city. You will find this vision in Zechariah 2:1-5. Let me quote a couple of verses. In the vision, an angel said to the man with the measuring line:

> ...Run, speak to this young man, saying, Jerusalem shall be inhabited as towns without walls for the multitude of men and cattle therein:
>
> For I, saith the Lord, will be unto her a wall of fire round about, and will be the glory in the midst of her.
>
> Zechariah 2:4,5 *KJV*

Oh, listen. Did you hear that word? It says the Lord will be *the* glory (definite article) in the midst of His people. This verse is not talking about glory in general or *a* glory. It is referring to *the* glory, meaning the Shekinah glory, the Presence of God. *The* glory will be in the midst of the restored Jerusalem!

God says, "When I build My work, I will build a wall and a hedge of fire. You won't need to build a human means of protection, for I will build a wall of fire about My work, and no one will tear it down. Internally, it will be filled with My Shekinah glory, which will give My people both a sense of purpose and of security."

Now, this message from God is exciting to me for several reasons. The Presence of God in His Body, the Church, the Shekinah glory that hovers over the ark of His covenant — this is the divining rod of any society. Whether or not a nation exists or prospers will not be decided by how clever the governing bodies are or how well they manage their economics. Rather, the determining factor is centered squarely in what the Church of Jesus Christ does within that nation. If any nation is to be spared — if healing and revival is to spread throughout the land — the Church must be on her knees in intercession.

May I say it this way? The decision is not being made in Washington D. C.; it is being made in the Church. I know people seldom believe that. It seems ridiculous! The people of God have always seemed kind of peculiar; outwardly they never look like the mighty of the earth. That is what the apostle Paul meant in First Corinthians 1:26,27:

> For you see your calling, brethren, that not many wise according to the flesh, not many mighty, not many noble, are called.
> But God has chosen the foolish things of the world to put to shame the wise, and God has chosen the weak things of the world to put to shame the things which are mighty.

Just look at yourself in the mirror, and you will see whom God has chosen. If that doesn't help you understand, just look at me. That will surely help you understand that God has chosen weak and despised things to confound the mighty!

Do you remember the occasion when two backslidden priests helped lead Israel into battle against the Philistines (1 Sam. 4:1-11)? The priests were Hophni and Phinehas, the sons of Eli. Both men were having sexual relations with women in the court, and neither had a heart for the things of God. They were involved in religion for formal reasons only. To them, it was merely a livelihood.

As the Israelites began to lose to the Philistines in the battle of Aphek, the elders of Israel said, "Bring the ark of the covenant out of the Holy of Holies." Thus, the ark of the covenant was transported to the battlefield. It was accompanied by Hophni and Phinehas, the two whose duty it was to protect the ark from such dishonor, for the elders' command had been born out of superstition rather than faith.

But superstition never spares anyone when God's judgment is upon the Church or upon an individual. A person may try to escape the consequences of his sin by carrying a Bible, wearing a cross, going to a church he hasn't gone to before, or practicing some religious formality, but none of these things in themselves will ever serve that purpose.

The judgment of God fell on Israel there at Aphek just as though the ark were not present. The Philistines routed the Israelites, and, in the process, they captured the ark.

The Philistines must have said, "Not only have we defeated Israel, we have captured their God!" They dragged the ark back to the city of Ashdod, where the temple to their own god Dagon was located.

Dagon was an interesting god, with the head of a man and the tail of a fish — in other words, a merman. You're probably ahead of me in the retelling of this story. The Philistines placed the ark of the covenant in front of Dagon. But when they came back the next morning, Dagon had fallen flat on his face! They set the idol upright again, but it was no use. The next morning, the Philistines found their "god" fallen face down once more, but this time the temple floor was scattered with broken pieces of Dagon! Meanwhile, the ark of the covenant just sat there shining in the midst of the carnage of a dethroned false god.

It is an interesting fact of archaeology that the Philistines never rebuilt this temple. They never again entered that building to worship their gods.

God also sent hemorrhoids and boils upon all the people of Ashdod. The people muttered, "We may have done the wrong thing" and sent the ark on to Gath, another Philistine city.

The people of Gath experienced the same thing: boils, hemorrhoids, and miserable pestilence. Finally, the Philistines said, "We have to get this ark out of our country!"

So they built themselves a special cart to carry the ark. Then just to see whether or not the God of Israel was really behind the terrible judgments that had been happening to them, the Philistines separated two milk cows that had recently given birth from their calves and yoked them together at the front of the cart.

Of course, we all know that a mother cow, when turned free, will immediately go back to her calf. But instead, those two milk cows independently pulled the cart containing the ark of the covenant directly toward Israel as the Philistines looked on in fear.

The Church of Jesus Christ is the ark of the covenant in contemporary society. It is the dwelling place of God. Therefore, what happens within a society is largely determined by what happens within the Church of Jesus Christ.

So God gives Zechariah this promise: "I am going to build a city without walls. I will place a wall of fire around it so enemies cannot come in, and I will send My Shekinah glory so that, internally, My Presence will be upon the people" (Zech. 2:4,5).

Then the Lord follows His promise with a warning.

> Ho, ho, come forth, and flee from the land of the north, saith the Lord: for I have spread you abroad as the four winds of the heaven, saith the Lord.
>
> Deliver thyself, O Zion, that dwellest with the daughter of Babylon.
>
> For thus saith the Lord of hosts; After the glory hath he sent me unto the nations which spoiled you: for he that toucheth you toucheth the apple of his eye.
>
> For, behold, I will shake mine hand upon them, and they shall be a spoil to their servants: and ye shall know that the Lord of hosts hath sent me.
>
> Zechariah 2:6-9 *KJV*

That warning was obviously God's word to His people who were still in Babylon. Many of the Jews in Babylon had become very prosperous. They had fared better in captivity than at home. They controlled the banks of Babylon and ran the truck farms. Some suspect that the Jews had a stranglehold on the economic and political life of both the Babylonian and later the Medio-Persian empires. On the whole, the Jews in exile were doing very well.

That's probably why only 50,000 Jews returned home with Ezra. When Cyrus issued his decree, he issued it to *all* the Jews in captivity: "Go home; here's money to build your temple and reestablish your land." Yet only 50,000 took Cyrus up on his offer. The rest liked Babylon too much to leave.

If I can interpret this warning in Zechariah's third vision, God was saying, "The tide of history has turned. The horns wherein authority has existed are going to be pounded to the earth, but My blessing is going to be upon My people.

"To those of you who have settled down in the land to which you've been scattered, I say *come home*. My hand is going to be upon those lands for judgment, so get out of Babylon. Get out of the Medo-Persian empire. Get out of those nations to which you've been scattered. My judgment is going to fall upon them, but I have returned to bless Jerusalem."

Ecclesiastes 2:26 is a similar and amazing scripture. It says, *"For God gives wisdom and knowledge and joy to a man who is good in His sight; but to the sinner He gives the work of gathering and collecting, that he may give to him who is good before God...."*

How specific should I be on this point? Are there not modern-day, divinely called believers who through discouragement have settled down to build their hopes through a fallen world system? Believers who dwell within Babylon in their hearts had better get out, for the judgment of God is ultimately upon this world system.

God has frequently turned the course of history. He is now preparing a Bride for His Son, who will in turn usher in the final acts of world history. The governments and economic powers of this earth are playing games with their last moments of borrowed time in the hourglass of God's eternity. I believe the move of God has already shifted from allowing the Babylons of this world to exist toward the specific building of His eternal Kingdom.

I believe that God will release untold amounts of land, property, and wealth to the cause of His Kingdom through the vehicle of the Church. He is issuing the call that, as His focus has changed, so His people's focus must also change.

What hope for security ultimately lies within the world system? To commit oneself to such an insubstantial hope is a foolish choice! The curtain is coming down.

I once enjoyed a close friendship with a well-known preacher and scholar named Willard Cantelon. He was uniquely called to Germany following World War II to preach reconciliation and to help build churches and Bible schools.

As a student, Willard Cantelon had always followed the economic markets of the world very thoroughly. He had in fact written and lectured frequently on the world monetary system. In a crusade following World War II, while he was raising money for the cause of Christ in Germany, a dear little lady came up to him at the end of the service one night and said, "My husband and I have saved money all our lives for the work of God, and we want you to have it all."

Willard said, "With tears in my eyes, I couldn't find it in my heart to tell that lady the truth: That very afternoon, the German government had totally devaluated the mark. What this dear woman was handing me was nothing but paper, worth no more than the value of putting it on the wall as wallpaper." (In fact, some people actually did paper their walls with the German mark after it was devaluated.)

This illustration speaks so eloquently to me. God told Zechariah, "Tell the people to get out of Babylon. Leave the lands to which I've scattered you, for I have again turned My face toward Jerusalem. I will build a hedge of fire around Jerusalem. I will put

My Shekinah glory within her. But you who have been scattered, leave those worldly systems in which you have been involved. Make priority choices that are in accord with spiritual things, not carnal, worldly things."

We must each allow the Holy Spirit to reveal to us what He is doing in this day. As Jesus frequently said, *"He that hath an ear, let him hear what the Spirit saith unto the churches"* (Rev. 3:6 *KJV*).

The sad truth is, despite God's warning, thousands of Jews died in captivity, refusing to return home even after God had once more turned His face toward Jerusalem. Similarly, hundreds of thousands of believers will be caught in Babylon when God's hand turns in judgment upon this world system.

Please allow me to add this personal prayer for you:

> Father, first of all, I want to thank You for the joy I feel in my spirit this very moment, the excitement of what You are doing in this day. Oh, God, the wall of fire is being built around Your program, and your Shekinah glory has moved in to dwell among Your people in a measure unknown throughout the past two thousand years of Church history. It is as though You are releasing every ounce of divine energy and power and every possible facility to your Church. You are empowering our hands for this final warfare, and that is so exciting!

> But, Father, I grieve in my spirit over those of us who have become such a part of Babylon while being forced to live in it. You've told us to be *in* the world, but not *of* the world. But too many of us have become so much a part of Babylon that we really can't respond to Your call: "Leave it; get out of it, for My hand is against it," saith the Lord.

> Finally, Father, I admit to You that I struggle with knowing what to say or how to say it to Your people. We have heard so many words; our ears and our hearts are full. One

more word piled on so many other words can become just so many words. Nevertheless, Lord, I pray that Your Holy Spirit would do His great and divine office work in the Name of Jesus Christ. Amen.

# CHAPTER 14

Everybody has roots somewhere; I guess mine are in Sharon, Pennsylvania. Dad was involved with the Pentecostal church there off and on for many years. His longest-term pastorate was in that town — a fortunate stint of thirteen years that got me through the ninth grade in one place.

How can I tell you about Sharon? The town was famous back then for Westinghouse Electric Company and for almost being the home of Sharon Steel. It was a wonderful mixture of cultures: Italian, Slovakian, and Irish, mixed in with those of us who were just somehow "Americans."

I loved my childhood. I walked to Wengler grade school and spent a ten-cent daily allowance at one of two wonderfully old-fashioned stores. I cut grass for our neighbors, the Robbs, and I worked for old Mr. Burchart stacking shelves, delivering groceries, and (YUCK!) cleaning his butchery machines. I became familiar with sawdust and the daily scrapings of butcher tables. Believe me, the seven dollars a week I received from Mr. Burchart was no gift!

I literally grew up in the back of the church (people called it an "attached parsonage"). I remember horrendous moments as a child when I had to go to the back of the church to turn out the lights right before a funeral, and someone was lying up front in a box!

There was a marvelous, old, water-logged basement in the church with a real coal bin. It had trunks filled with old clothes, discarded linens, and the miscellany of a preacher's travels through life.

My memories include crisp and fragrant autumns, burning leaves, walks through Pine Hollow, and the noisy yells of Friday night football crowds. I also remember a barber who cut hair in the back room of his home, as well as the surrounding homes of people whose lives helped make up the mosaic of my childhood background.

Then there was Jerry and Joyce, Tom and Dick, Leroy and Ernie and Dutch. I came of age there on Stambaugh Avenue. I discovered the use of my adolescent body, and, although I wouldn't have known the word masturbation, I sure discovered the process.

I had my first peek at pornography in the attic of a friend's home as we rustled through his soldier brother's gear. And who can forget being taught to kiss by Carole and Nancy? They had just seen a Doris Day film with Gordon MacRae the night before. They decided that, since I wasn't allowed to attend movies, they needed to prepare me for the real world. Who can measure the sweetness or startle of a first kiss? It was especially wonderful being taught to do it right with all the accompanying "MacRae-like" actions.

Carole Sherwood was my first real sweetheart. Red-haired and sharp-witted, she and her family provided an alternative to my rather parochial view of life. Her father Joe and his wife really loved me. They took me for my first speedboat ride on Conneaut Lake and provided me with my first attempt at water-skiing. They were sensitive to my parents' restrictions, yet they always broadened my sights a little each time I came to their home.

It was at the Sherwoods while playing badminton that I looked on, horrified, as little boys threw kerosene on a trash fire in a driveway behind their home. Unmindful of the danger, I dashed after one of the little running fires and grabbed him, extinguishing the flame.

All the boys survived, although two were burned severely. However, something had happened in me during the process. For some reason, this was an encounter with life that jarred my own sensitivity. It was my first personal contact with a tragic accident involving other people. I was not only shaken, but I discovered an octave that echoed into my own past. (As a toddler, I had experienced a tragic accident of my own, resulting in the loss of one eye.)

In the years that followed, I would experience separations, dangers, and frustrations. But that incident still seems somehow to mark the death of innocence for me. Shortly after that, the attachments to my childhood chums fell away. I was growing up — wobbly, loud, and insecure, but growing up nonetheless.

Junior high school was the breaking point in my young life. My school was located in downtown Sharon near the Shenango River (a river that conveniently overflowed every year and gave us at least one serendipitous vacation!).

Who can explain those middle years? There was the memorable time I took my first "gang shower" after gym class with boys who were making a career of eighth and ninth grade! There was the trauma of losing my tight-knit identity of neighborhood school chums as I surrendered unceremoniously to the world of middle-school mayhem. Adolescence in general is hard enough, but junior high school should be outlawed!

There were also changes going on in me — not only in body hair (which was always too little and sparsely scattered) or in reproductive development, but in attitude. I ran the radio for the principal and began to play the sousaphone in the junior high band. The sousaphone weighed twenty-seven pounds, about a fourth of my total weight, but my instructor said he could tell by my developing hips that I would ultimately "be able to bear it."

All I remember was going away from that conversation feeling proud that at least my hips were testifying to my growth. "Good news, tonight, folks — I'm going to have wide hips!"

# CHAPTER 15

A friend once introduced me to his congregation by calling me "an iconoclast." It was his way of safely separating himself from my somewhat bombastic and hard-hitting style of ministry. Some friends have called that style prophetic; others have had more harsh descriptions.

When I heard my friend's description of me, I said to myself, *An iconoclast, huh? That's someone who blows up icons. All right, I can identify with that.*

After all, Gideon's first divine instructions were to throw down an altar. Interestingly, the greatest reaction to that incident was *not* from Israel's captors but from the fearful, submissive fellow believers in Gideon's own tribe!

My earliest ministry was evangelistic and prophetic. I loved the new, the young, and the radical. When my denomination sent me forth to defend its positions to the college youth of the '60s, I found myself instead revitalized by the commitment of these college students and came back to identify their causes to the denominational leadership.

That was not smart! The denomination sent out the message afterward that nothing was to be learned from "the rioters." This experience left me inevitably wary of institutions, particularly Christian ones.

I could have never fashioned nor dreamed of a life like the one I would ultimately live. I spent fourteen years teaching in an institutional college and thirty years in pastoral pursuit of restoration involving a denominational icon that was more than forty years old when I first stumbled on the scene. Was this how I was meant to live my life?

Agents of restoration don't normally volunteer. (Of course, I doubt that a volunteer line exists in Heaven, nor are there predestinarian forces that command obeisance.) There's no decent drafting program, nor is there any on-the-field training. Actually, the task of restoration is a little bit like love and marriage — better explained in the doing. But everyone who receives a divine "push" into that task ultimately seizes the opportunity like a lifeline and holds on with the tenacity of a bulldog.

Two such agents of destiny by the names of Zerubbabel and Joshua were assigned to the original moments of Israel's restoration from seventy years of Babylonian captivity. Both were very human men, "captivity babies" who had been born, educated, and raised far from the hopes and aspirations of the people of God. They had never known the grandeur of the temple. They had never known the time when God's people had been at their best.

So when God's mantle dropped upon Zerubbabel and Joshua to lead this first return from captivity, the endeavor seemed bound to fail. It meant going back into the heart of opposition to do something no one really wanted to see done — especially these two men whose humanity had formerly demonstrated vulnerability, weakness, and, in the case of Joshua, defilement.

You see, in many ways Zerubbabel and Joshua were failures — men who hadn't made it in life; men who had great destiny but little achievement. Nevertheless, the mantle of God had come upon them. The ultimate issue of restoration, therefore, was to get Zerubbabel and Joshua "off their duff" to return to the job God had placed in their hands.

At a crucial point, the prophet Zechariah spoke a word from the Lord to these two men. Zechariah said, "I saw a vision, and in this vision I saw a great candlestick" (Zech. 4:1-3).

The candlestick the prophet described was immediately recognizable to Zerubbabel and Joshua. It was the seven-pronged menorah, which was the temple or the tabernacle lampstand. However, the menorah in the vision was uniquely different than any they had ever seen before. Although it had seven lamps as did all the menorahs of the tabernacle and temple, this candlestick had a great golden reservoir filled with oil in the center of it. In addition, seven golden pipes went from this reservoir to each of the seven lamps.

Now that was amazing in itself, for normally each lamp of the temple and tabernacle menorahs had only its personal provision that had to be daily changed and refilled. But the vision didn't stop there. Alongside the menorah, Zechariah also saw two stately olive trees that served as living sources of oil. These two olive trees also had golden pipes connecting them to this golden reservoir (v. 12).

That meant, of course, that this lampstand would never be without light. No one had to run to it to provide fresh oil, for there were two living suppliers from which oil constantly flowed into this golden bowl. In turn, the oil in the golden bowl flowed into each of the seven lamps, thus causing them to be entirely, totally, and continually provided with a fresh supply of oil.

Zechariah himself was overwhelmed by the vision. He had never seen a menorah like that before, and he had no idea what it meant. So the prophet asked the angel of God, "What does this unusual lampstand mean?"

The angel answered, *"...This is the word of the Lord unto Zerubbabel, saying, Not by might, nor by power, but by my spirit, saith the Lord of hosts"* (Zech. 4:6 *KJV*).

Then the angel continued, saying in essence, "What is this mountain, this difficulty, this opposition? For unto Zerubbabel it shall be as though it did not exist" (v. 7).

Zechariah also asked the angel, "What are these two olive trees that stand next to the lampstand with pipes that connect them to the reservoir of oil?"

Again the angel answered the prophet with a very unique word: "These are the two sons of fatness or of oil — the sons of anointing who stand by the candlestick" (v. 14).

Listen carefully, my friend — God has an eternal commitment to work through individuals. Five times in Zechariah 4, the job God wants done is personalized by the name of Zerubbabel. And if you go back to the previous chapter, you'll find that the job God wants done is five times personalized by the name of Joshua.

I have news for you: We live in an existential world following two world wars that have brought both a psychological and a philosophical disillusionment that modern man has been unable to eradicate. In this humanistic society, so many drift through life like a cork in a slow-moving river. People are told, "You're a cog in a machine, just a part of the action. You do your little thing, and then you die. The world goes on without you; no one needs you."

In contrast, God says, "Every job in My Kingdom is personalized. It's Mary's job; it's John's job; it's Jim's job; it's Sue's job. Everything I do is expressed in terms of a person. Further, each person can accomplish the task I assign to him or her only by means of My grace."

# CHAPTER 16

The entire illustration of the candlestick centers around oil, which is a frequent biblical symbol of the Holy Spirit. This may be the only picture in the Bible that presents us with a perfect circle. The supply of the oil and the oil that is being burnt to provide light is all part of one cycle in which no one from the outside is involved.

God simply declares that these olive trees are the two anointed ones. Who are these anointed ones? Zerubbabel and Joshua — two incredibly human vessels.

You may ask, "But isn't the whole idea of the lampstand to encourage Zerubbabel and Joshua to get the job done?" That's right.

"Isn't that why God tells them that His Spirit is actually the One who is going to do it? Isn't that what the angel meant when he said Zerubbabel would cry out as he finished the work, 'Grace, grace unto the cornerstone'?" (Zech. 4:7). Yes — but only in a way.

The vision of the candlestick that God reveals in the book of Zechariah is only truly fulfilled in the New Testament. A person becomes a complete cycle of capability as he is surrendered to the Holy Spirit. Both the supply and the release — the reservoir and the burning, the energy and the supply for the energy — are within that transformed life as the Holy Spirit fills, floods, and enables.

No man ever need look outside for a source of strength; no woman ever need look somewhere else for the ability to do a job. You see, as God has called, He has given the Word. His Word is the power to accomplish the task. The word of the Lord unto Zerubbabel is His message to every believer: "This mountain *shall* be moved — not by might, nor by power, but by My Spirit."

I have often asked myself, "Why is it that God's people are not doing God's job? Why is it that most Christians are sidelined?"

It plagues me. In this most strategic hour of history, how can people who name the Name of Christ act as though Jesus is never going to come? They act as though building homes and having shops and going to work is "where it's at."

I've rehearsed this in my mind. Some of us act like we've been "red-shirted." In other words, we think God has put us on the back bench for some future time of involvement. I think the principal reason for this is that a lot of us have been sidetracked by the guilt and condemnation of the enemy.

The prophet Samuel has been a neglected Old Testament character in Bible stories. Look into his life. Samuel experienced tragic circumstances within his family. All we know is that both of his sons grew up to be exactly like the sons of Eli — worthless men who had sexual relations with the women of the court while occupying the positions of priests unto God. Their immorality and abuse of their sacred office provide an unthinkable chapter in the chronicle of the prophet Samuel's long life.

So many Christians, when faced with this kind of tragedy and especially when aided by some of the teaching that abounds in the Church today, would say, "All right, Samuel, you've failed in the arena of parenting, so you're relegated to the sidelines. Sit this one out!"

Instead, Samuel came to God, and the Spirit of God anointed him to be the architect of the new era of Israel's destiny. Samuel personally inaugurated the theocratic monarchy, a type of the coming reign of the Messiah, that came straight from the heart of God. Samuel personally established the school of the prophets and turned Israel from a culture of the judges to a kingdom under the principles of God. The prophet accomplished all this in spite of his personal failure and disillusionment.

I don't know what is going to be recorded about the failure of Samuel at the Judgment Seat of Christ. Maybe he was a bad father. Maybe he was so involved in the things of God that he neglected his own family. There is a lot to be said about that possibility. On the other hand, perhaps he simply had two sons who exercised their free will to do their own thing as they grew to adulthood. How can any of us know? This I do believe: Samuel had the courage to live as a man of God in spite of failure.

If you are sidelined from doing God's will because of personal failure, you need to restudy the principles of restoration. It is not your nature that has brought you to God's purpose, nor is it your attractiveness. God has called you to do a job; God has applied your name to that job; and God says to you, "It is the word of the Lord to you that will enable you to do the job — *if* you will move with it and do something about it."

Many want to sit and "cry in their milk" the rest of their lives. These are the people who go into eternity with empty hands. They sideline themselves by listening to the enemy rather than by hearing the word of the Lord.

David, whom the Bible calls "a man after God's own heart," was a man of sensuous passion, high emotion, and, ultimately, despicable sin. Perhaps even worse than his actual adulterous acts was his despicable weakness in having Uriah, the cuckolded husband of an adulterous wife, Bathsheba, killed in the battle to cover his sin. David certainly paid for that.

When it came time for the building of the temple, David said to God, "I want to do this for You."

And God said, "You're a man of blood; you can't build the temple."

At that point, most of us would have sidelined ourselves for the rest of our lives. "I'm out of the race. Just listen to what God said to me!" we'd tell people as we sat around, paralyzed by discouragement.

Churches are filled with people who have been sidelined because of something that happened in their past. Perhaps a particular failure or tragic event stumbled their faith, or maybe someone did or said something that offended them or hurt their feelings. Whatever the cause, these people have been sitting on the sidelines ever since!

But David didn't respond that way to his failure. Instead, he said, "All right, God, I understand. I know the wages of sin is death. I know the soul that sins shall surely die. I know that You won't be mocked and if a man sows to his flesh, he of his flesh reaps corruption. I know all that. But, God, I'm not going to be sidelined by this. You put my name on a job, and I'm going to do it."

God so loved what He saw in David that He gave David the entire architecture of the temple; then God let him gather all the materials for the temple's construction. Most people don't understand that Solomon was, after all, only the building contractor. David was the one who was given the temple in his heart. And until the day David died, he was on the front line, *building*.

# CHAPTER 17

It was a summer afternoon in 1979, and I was back at Lake Erie, walking the shoreline of the lake that touches Erie, Pennsylvania. I had come back to western Pennsylvania from the West Coast because my dad was dying.

My brother Bob now pastored a church that had been started in Erie many years before by a young colleague of mine named David. David and I, along with our girlfriends, had held the first prayer meetings that led to this fine new church. After David's tragic death and other intervening circumstances, my brother took over the pastorate there.

Going back to Erie was weird and nostalgic. I was haunted by so many specters there. My favorite uncle had lived there, and a favorite cousin had drowned there. I had my first crush there on another cousin and spent a night getting sick on strawberries with two other cousins in the attic of my aunt's home in nearby Wesleyville. I still can't stand the sight of them (I mean the strawberries, not the cousins!).

An uncle who was a policeman had been gunned down in Erie. In fact, I had attended so many funerals there that I thought it was the town's chief reason for being! Besides funerals, I had also attended many Brady reunions in Erie or in Conneaut, where I saw all the other odd people who claimed to be related to me.

I don't think my brother and his new friends had any idea what was going on inside me the weekend of my visit. My thoughts were full of memories of my friend David, who had moved to Erie from Florida. I had slept at his home, eaten with him, double-dated with him, preached with him, and given him the bachelor party before he and Sandy married.

The primitive prayer meetings David and I held had been in an old Victorian home piled high with memorabilia and the smell of newspapers and cats. At the time, I was dating Joyce from Conneaut while attending college in Grove City. Every weekend I'd drive the sixty miles from Grove City to Conneaut — and then on to Erie for those inevitable prayer meetings.

But that wasn't the major specter from my past I had to confront that weekend. Bob took me downtown to the Hammond hospital to visit an old anachronism of my father's ministry and of my life, a man named Harry Shadow. I knew this would be another time for me to be called "Ricky" and reminded of my childhood years. That was all right, though; I didn't mind. It was what Bob announced — rather callously, I thought — as we drove into the hospital parking lot that hit me hard.

"You know, this is where you lost your eye," Bob said matter-of-factly. "The folks sure had some rough days around this place." I'm sure my parents must have told me at one time or another where the incident Bob was talking about occurred; it just didn't register in my mind. Until that moment, I had assumed it happened in a different city.

As our visit with Harry went on, I eventually left Bob in the room. He always was better than I ever was at that type of pastoral duties. I walked outside and studied the hospital as if I expected to find something to explain what had taken place so many years earlier.

It had happened the summer of 1940. As a denominational superintendent, Dad had been called to fill in at a Washington D. C. church that was in between pastors. After several months of loneliness, Dad asked his wife to come to Washington D. C. on the train. Since I was only two years old, I went along with Mom, although I honestly can't remember a thing about the trip.

The church family who had provided housing for Dad simply adjusted their facilities to accommodate two more guests. Their own children were raised, but they managed to find a discarded tricycle in the attic for the newly arrived toddler to play with. Time or abuse had eliminated the rubber handle grip.

Then one day I had a tragic accident. I fell while riding the tricycle and rammed my left eye into the exposed chrome bar.

I only know what I've been told. Doctors in Washington tried to save the eye, but, ultimately, the case was transferred a hospital closer to my parents' home in Conneaut, Ohio. It was there that the decision was finally made to surgically remove the damaged eye.

Strange that something so ultimately consuming in my life, so directional and life-forming, was hardly ever mentioned. Here I was, forty years later, walking for the first time on grounds where my parents had striven with their difficult choice and, doubtless, their faith.

My loss of an eye was an omnipresent issue throughout my childhood. The annual trips to Cleveland for new "glass eyes" and the constant warnings — "Remember, you're not like other boys; you only have one eye" — still abound in my memory. I remember running up a snowy hill to terrified parents with my empty eye socket bleeding from a sledding accident. I remember the endless fear I experienced as I grew up, wondering whether I could ever learn to care for myself. Could I ever really be independent?

Yes, it was all there. But somehow the issue had been cordoned off in silence and lived out in the secret emptiness of my fears and insecurities. How could I ever have forgotten Erie?

# CHAPTER 18

There is a saying heard a great deal around the time of various championship games such as the Superbowl: *"There is no game tomorrow."* In other words, that means "Don't spare your quarterback in reserve and don't coddle the weakness of some veteran player's injury, because there won't be another opportunity after this one. This is it. It's all decided today."

In a way, that is the issue of Zechariah 3. There is no getting to tomorrow. If the issue of Zechariah 3 isn't settled, there isn't a game. It may well be the greatest of issues facing the believer. Certainly it seems to be the greatest of all issues in the gauntlet of overcoming and victorious Christianity.

Allow me to quote the entirety of the third chapter of Zechariah, which relates his fourth vision. The chapter is really quite short, but we need to read it together, for it provides our instruction for the rest of this book. Please don't read ahead without first reading these words. It would even be helpful to read them aloud in order to anchor the words in your heart and mind.

Then he showed me Joshua the high priest standing before the angel of the Lord, and Satan standing at his right hand to accuse him.

And the Lord said to Satan, "The Lord rebuke you, Satan! Indeed, the Lord who has chosen Jerusalem rebuke you! Is this not a brand plucked from the fire?"

Now Joshua was clothed with filthy garments and standing before the angel.

And he spoke and said to those who were standing before him saying, "Remove the filthy garments from him." Again he said to him, "See, I have taken your iniquity away from you and will clothe you with festal robes."

Then I said, "Let them put a clean turban on his head." So they put a clean turban on his head and clothed him with garments, while the angel of the Lord was standing by.

And the angel of the Lord admonished Joshua saying,

"Thus says the Lord of hosts, 'If you will walk in My ways, and if you will perform My service, then you will also govern My house and also have charge of My courts, and I will grant you free access among these who are standing here.

'Now listen, Joshua the high priest, you and your friends who are sitting in front of you — indeed they are men who are a symbol, for behold, I am going to bring in My servant the Branch.

'For behold, the stone that I have set before Joshua; on one stone are seven eyes. Behold, I will engrave an inscription on it,' declares the Lord of hosts, 'and I will remove the iniquity of that land in one day.

'In that day,' declares the Lord of hosts, 'every one of you will invite his neighbor to sit under his vine and under his fig tree.'"

Zechariah 3:1-10 *NAS*

We have discussed the background of Zechariah, but it is important at this point to do some review. Judah had been taken into captivity in three successive waves. Daniel was in the first wave to go into captivity; Ezekiel in the second; and then, finally, Jerusalem itself was destroyed. From the first wave of captivity, the period of time was seventy years. Of course, all Israel went into captivity.

That so-called "Babylonian captivity" is one of several key illustrations of divine Providence. The judgment of God is a consequence of sin, even when the sin is committed by His own people. However, remember that God has a beneficial purpose in judgment. He means to restore His people to their divine purpose.

All this is indeed the background of the book of Zechariah. Zerubbabel and Joshua had led 50,000 captive Jews back to their homeland to begin rebuilding the temple. They had begun to rebuild with an evangelistic fervor. But when opposition arose from within and without, the building of the temple was brought to a halt. For sixteen long years, the sacred cause, the first purpose of God, lay unfinished. The begun-but-unfinished temple was an incomplete shadow, a mocking charade against Jehovah God.

Finally, the aged Haggai — a prophet from the past, weary but committed — found a voice. With harsh and persistent insistence, he urged the people to quit building their homes and to stop doing their own thing so they could get back to the job to which God had called them. Haggai's moral courage and stamina inspired the much younger Zechariah, a more positive and exciting voice. Zechariah began to take his stand on the cause of rebuilding the temple after Haggai's third month of message.

It was not until five months *after* Zechariah had the courage to stand up for the prophetic issue of restoring the temple that God opened the door of prophetic revelation to him. In one long January night, Zechariah received revelations that place him among the most complete and panoramic prophets of all time. This third chapter that we look at now begins the fourth and, in many ways, the most significant vision. It certainly contains the key message of this book.

Look at the phrase that begins Zechariah 3: *"Then he* [the Lord] *showed me...."* When I see that phrase, I want to bow my heart before the sovereign Lord of eternal harvest, the Commander-in-

Chief of sacred warfare, and pray that He would somehow show us this lesson.

It's one thing for a minister to have a burden on his heart for a particular message and to agonize over its delivery. But it's quite another thing for people to leave a service (or the chapter of a book, for that matter) revolutionized, changed, and reordered. Too many Christians go to church complacently singing, "Another Sunday, Another Service" (to the tune of "Another Opening, Another Show") when, in fact, the anointing must be as exacting on the hearer or the reader as it is on the preacher or the author.

What is this fourth vision given to Zechariah? First of all, it is personified in Joshua the young high priest. Remember, Joshua had been born in captivity. So even though he was in the order of high priests, he had never even seen the original temple! He was the son and grandson of a high priest, a necessary pedigree according to the Law. Suddenly and without preparation, Joshua was assigned a role in leading the people of God back to Jerusalem.

In this vision, Joshua stands before the angel of the Lord. Certainly this is not judgment. Satan has no right before God in reference to the judgment of God's people. All the enemy can do is try to reach an out-of-court settlement! Of course, he's busy doing that all the time. Although he has no official right in the actual judgment of a believer, Satan is constantly trying to make a deal.

You'll notice in Zechariah 3 that there is no judgment throne. The three players are all standing. Also notice that the terms "Lord" and "angel of the Lord" are interchangeably used. There is little doubt that this is no regular angel, but the Lord Himself.

So here they stand — Joshua, the returned high priest; Satan; and the Lord. Never is there a doubt about Satan's purpose, especially when it has to do with God's people. Satan is the accuser. His name means *adversary* or *accuser*; his title "devil" or "diabolos" means *slanderer*. The names fit well, for accusing and slandering is exactly what the enemy is always doing.

We don't know what Satan is saying in the vision, for that information isn't given here. But a guess isn't difficult because verse 4 tells us Joshua is standing in filthy or "excrement-bespattered" garments. Knowing the devil's typical accusation, I have a pretty good idea of what this is all about.

> **And the Lord said to Satan, "The Lord rebuke** [and continually rebuke] **you, Satan! The Lord who** [now and habitually] **has chosen Jerusalem rebuke you! Is this not a brand plucked from the fire?"**
>
> Zechariah 3:2

It's hard for most of us to understand that our standing in God is based on His irrevocable call or election. The call of God is without and beyond repentance, and the election of God has to do with the standard He originated before the foundation of the earth — namely, that those who trust in the blood atonement of Christ would be approved. That's what divine election means; that is our place of security.

God says in rebuking Satan, "I now choose Jerusalem [the literal Hebrew verse reads, "I now choose and have habitually chosen, or continue to choose, Jerusalem"], and I rebuke you, Satan!"

Our standing as believers is that we are *in Christ*; we are not judged according to our works until the Judgment Seat of Christ. The next action in this scenario speaks volumes. The Lord says to the angels standing before Him, "Strip those dirty, filthy robes off him," and the angels obey. In a moment, the angels begin dressing Joshua in lovely, ceremonially cleaned robes. So God acknowledges the filthy garments; He doesn't explain them away, nor does He treat them as irrelevant. Instead, He immediately acts in grace to end the dilemma.

The young prophet Zechariah becomes so excited watching this vision that he can't stay off the stage. As the angels are putting fine robes on the disabled Joshua, Zechariah jumps into the middle of the vision and says, "Hey, put a turban on his head too!" According to Zechariah's word, the angels put a turban on Joshua's head as the Lord stands by and watches.

Each of these issues we will deal with in succeeding chapters. But the simple revelation of the story in itself is revolutionary.

Following these events, the word of the Lord comes to the now cleansed, reclothed, and reauthorized Joshua. God says, "If you will obey My ways and keep My charges, I will give you the rule over My house. I will also give you access to My courts and cause you and those who sit with you [meaning the other priests] to stand in My very Presence."

The Lord goes on to say something incredible to Joshua: "Don't you understand that you are all but types or shadows of that great Priest who shall come — namely, the Branch or the Messiah?"[8]

Then the angel of the Lord says something that is equally interesting. I believe most Bible commentators miss this point entirely. The Lord declares, *"'For behold, the stone that I have laid before Joshua: upon the stone are seven eyes* [or facets of the sevenfold radiations of the Spirit of God]. *Behold, I will engrave its inscription,'"* says the Lord of hosts, *'And I will remove the iniquity of that land in one day'"* (Zech. 3:9).

Now, most commentators say this is an expression only of the Messiah. I don't believe so. God doesn't mix His metaphors. The Messiah has already been referred to prophetically in this passage. This verse and Daniel 9 are both speaking about the Church — that stone of which the Messiah is the chief cornerstone. And it is this stone that is set before Joshua.

Notice how God ends the prophecy. Remember, the Israelites had been building their own homes and pursuing their own self-interests. The entire message of Haggai had basically been "Quit doing your own thing, and get on with the job God has for you."

---

[8]Author's paraphrase of Zechariah 3:6-8.

But now Zechariah hears the Lord saying, "And in that day I'll give you a house. You'll be able to invite your neighbors over and have them sit under your own fig tree" (v. 10).

Isn't that amazing? I love the way the Lord does that! No one ever responds to the call of God without receiving His grace and sufficiency. God is a wonderful Provider. For instance, when David desired to build a house for God, God's response was "I'll build a house for you!"

So what are the specific, personal, important, and critical revelations of this vision?

In cinematography, there is the moment for the "close-up" or the "stop-action" camera shot. Let's apply that same concept to this study as we isolate several significant points. Let's come up close to these points and see their relevance — particularly how the Holy Spirit will apply them to us. As one writer said, "Statesmanship is the art of finding out in what direction Almighty God is going, and in getting things out of His way."

# CHAPTER 19

The biblical account of the temple restoration project clearly shows us some things we have to get out of the way if we're not going to be a stumbling block to God's plan in *this* generation.

In Alexander MacClaren's *Expositions of Holy Scripture* concerning Zechariah, he says this: "Zechariah worked side by side with Haggai to quicken the religious life of the people, and thus to remove the gravest hindrances to the work of rebuilding the Temple." MacClaren goes on to say, "Inward indifference, not outward opposition, is the real reason for slow progress in God's work, and prophets who see visions and preach repentance are the true practical men."[9]

Some things bear repeating. To accurately interpret this vision in Zechariah 3, it is imperative that we understand why Joshua is standing before the Lord in filthy garments. Joshua was a mere mortal, a sinner, just as all men are sinners through whom God works.

---

[9]Dr. Alexander MacClaren, *Expositions of Holy Scripture* (Grand Rapids, Michigan: Wm. B. Eerdmans Publishing Co., 1932), p. 280.

As Paul the apostle wrote, *"For I know that in me (that is, in my flesh,) dwelleth no good thing..."* (Rom. 7:18 *KJV*).

Young Joshua had made a tragically critical error as high priest of the people: He had allowed the returning captives to intermarry with the people of the land. This was against God's purpose and ultimately brought a great judgment upon the people of Israel. Ezra 10 is all about the mistake Joshua made, the consequences of which continued for many years.

So Joshua wasn't a perfect man. I'm sure that as he stands before God in the vision, some of the filthiness on his garments are of his own making. But Joshua's shortcomings are not the entire reason we find him in this place.

The significance of this story is that Joshua stands before the Lord in a *representative* capacity. You see, for a high priest to stand before God in defiled garments would have been his death. Not only did the garments have to be pure from the viewpoint of the fuller (who was the ancient version of a modern "dry cleaner"), but they also had to be ceremonially cleansed and anointed before the priest could wear them into the Presence of God. But here Joshua stands in filthy — or, as we have learned, "excrement-bespattered" — garments.

In a sense, Joshua wears these robes as certainly as he would have worn the sacramental robes of purity. He is the high priest of the people, so it is imperative that he come before God with the sins and the needs of the people upon his shoulders. Thus, what is happening in Zechariah 3 is not simply a judgment of Joshua. As is always the case, Satan's attack is aimed at not just one individual; he wants to bring an accusation against the *entire* covenant people of God.

The enemy is saying, "God, these people are worthless. How can You continue to work through these 'covenant people,' as You call them, when they are filthy and perverse and they continue to disobey You?"

Representation may well be one of the most critical things we will ever learn. After all, this man Joshua was a type of Jesus Christ. In a sense, Joshua represented what Jesus did for us in reference to sin. Paul says to the Corinthians concerning Jesus, *"For He made Him who knew no sin to be sin for us, that we might become the righteousness of God in Him"* (2 Cor. 5:21).

This verse gives us insight into Jesus' prayer in the Garden of Gethsemane. Sweating great drops as it were of blood, Jesus cried out to the Father in anguish, "Oh, Father, if it be possible, let this cup pass from Me!"

I have heard some teach that Jesus was crying for deliverance from His impending death on the Cross. Indeed, it would be hard to describe the horrible ignominy and the excruciating agony of death by crucifixion. There has probably never been a form of capital punishment in the history of the world more inhumane than the one Jesus had to endure. Crucifixion often required days to produce death. This meant the criminal was often suspended in excruciating pain for days, although sometimes his legs were broken to facilitate a quicker end.

Crucifixion was surely a horrible thing, but I believe it is totally wrong to suggest that Jesus, fearing the suffering of the Cross, cried out, "Father, let this cup pass from Me!" *No, Jesus was talking about the cup that only He could drink — the cup that contained our sins.*

The pure, sinless Son of God had never once by volitional choice offended the will of the Father. He had always pleased the Father. Indeed, His very words had continually been controlled by the Holy Spirit who had descended upon Him in His human flesh. By the Spirit of God, Jesus had been given the courage and strength to be conformed perfectly to the Father's will.

Thus, Jesus knew that the fellowship He had always known with the Father — His perfect, unbroken harmony with the Father's will — would be broken as He Himself became sin. That is why Jesus would cry out in His agony from the Cross, "My God, why have

You forsaken Me?" The Father had to turn His back on His own Son, who in that moment took upon Himself the vileness of our sin nature.

Think of all the dregs of human nature that you know about. Think of the worst about yourself and the worst about people who have lived through the ages. Mix all that in a concoction of unbelievable abomination, and then realize that *Christ had to drink it.* This is the amazing truth Paul gives us when he says, *"For He made Him who knew no sin to be sin for us, that we might become the righteousness of God in Him"* (2 Cor. 5:21).

Perhaps this is the most essential teaching of the Christian Gospel. There is no doctrinal or church position that is greater than this teaching. It is essential to understand that a transference occurred with Jesus' death on the Cross. Our sin became His; His righteousness became ours. It was a transference of natures, a true imputation.

Joshua was a man like us. No divinity existed in him at all, other than the spirit of man that had proceeded from the breath of God. Joshua was exactly like you and me; yet he was willing to stand before God on behalf of other men. He was a priest, and he understood his priesthood.

Derek Prince, an English scholar who became an American preacher, wrote an incredibly important book. It was ultimately transcribed into the congressional record of both the House and the Senate of the United States. The title is *Shaping History Through Prayer and Fasting.*

Prince writes: "God has vested in us — His believing people on earth — authority by which we may determine the destinies of nations and governments. He expects us to use our authority both for His glory and for our own good. If we fail to do so, we are answerable for the consequences."[10]

---

[10]Derek Prince, *Shaping History Through Prayer and Fasting* (Old Tappan, New Jersey: Fleming H. Revell Co., 1973), p. 26.

That statement brings us to Zechariah 3 with a renewed sense of understanding. Remember for a moment the call of God on an earlier young Jeremiah. Jeremiah immediately did what most of us do — he said, "Oh, Lord, surely not me! I'm young; I'm ineffective!" (Jer. 1:6).

God must have a marvelous sense of humor when He calls people. You must also remember the calling of Gideon. Gideon was so fearful that he probably threshed his grain in the middle of the night so the Midianites wouldn't see him. On top of that, he crawled down into a pit where grapes were pressed to make wine so he would be doubly sure that no enemy could see him. Can you imagine the angel of God coming in the middle of the night to this fearful man and shouting down into the pit, "Hello, Gideon, thou mighty man of valor!" (Judges 6:12). What a sense of humor God has!

When Jeremiah was finished protesting that he was too young and incapable of fulfilling God's call, the Lord said to him, *"See, I have this day set you over the nations and over the kingdoms, to root out and to pull down, to destroy and to throw down, to build and to plant"* (Jer. 1:10).

Look at those incredible words. More than 2,500 years have passed through history since that word from God was given to Jeremiah, and it has come true just as God said it would. In Jeremiah 1:9, God tells him why: *"...Behold, I have put My words in your mouth."* God's words in Jeremiah's mouth had the power to root out, pull down, build up, and literally change the course of nations.

You see, Jeremiah stood in a twofold relationship. On one hand, he was a subject of Judah in submission to a local kingdom. His first message of prophecy was to tell his people that this natural kingdom was going to cease to exist.

But Jeremiah was a dual citizen, for he was also a member of God's Kingdom. God had elevated him through prophetic ministry to a place of authority over the very rulers to whom he was in subjection under a natural plan. In other words, in the realm of the Spirit, Jeremiah was prophetically over those to whom he was in subjection as a natural citizen. Isn't that incredible? Jeremiah's prophetic ministry made him one who would rule, throw down, build up, and replant kingdoms and powers.

That's what we all are. We are first citizens of a natural human kingdom. The Bible is filled with our responsibility as Christians to submit to that natural kingdom. But we are dual citizens! By spiritual rebirth, through faith in Jesus Christ, we are also citizens of God's Kingdom and citizens of Heaven.

Jesus Christ said to the Church, *"Do not fear, little flock, for it is your Father's good pleasure to give you the kingdom"* (Luke 12:32). Concerning Jesus, it was said, *"The Lord has established His throne in heaven, and His kingdom rules over all"* (Ps. 103:19).

Ephesians 1:20-22 declares that Jesus Christ has had all powers and authorities put under His feet. In that same chapter, Paul prays for the Church:

> That the God of our Lord Jesus Christ, the Father of glory, may give to you the spirit of wisdom and revelation in the knowledge of Him,
>
> the eyes of your understanding being enlightened; THAT YOU MAY KNOW....
>
> Ephesians 1:17,18

That we may know what? How great Jesus is? That has already been said. What then does Paul want us to know? He tells us in verses 18-20:

> ...That you may know what is the hope of His calling, what are the riches of the glory of His inheritance in the saints,
>
> and what is the exceeding greatness of His power toward us who believe, according to the working of His mighty power
>
> which He worked in Christ when He raised Him from the dead....

Christ's power is still the authority over this universe, and the same power that raised Him from the dead now works in the believer — that very same power!

Look at this incredible scripture in First Corinthians 2: *"But as it is written: 'Eye has not seen, nor ear heard, nor have entered into the heart of man the things which God has prepared for those who love Him'"* (v. 9).

Most of us know that verse well. But do you know what verse 12 of that same chapter says? It says, *"Now we have received, not the spirit of the world, but the Spirit who is from God, that we might know the things that have been freely given to us by God."*

How incredible is the lie Satan has told about us! Paul says, "It is my heart desire that you believers would suddenly have not the spirit of the world, but that the Spirit of God would reveal to you the things freely given to us by Christ."

Christians often live like paupers and beggars when they are actually King's kids. Most believers I talk to think they are somehow the pawns of the decisions made in Washington or on Wall Street. Perhaps they even view what goes on in the United Nations as "the ultimate."

Yet God says, *"You* are the ones who are going to make the decisions for the world. I have given this authority to you, and the Spirit of God is the One who will give you understanding of the things that are in this earthly realm." This is in effect what the Word is saying!

You need to know that this principle has never been changed. When God made man, He gave him dominion over the earth. Of course, we know that through the fall — through disobedience, the entrance of sin, and the accepting of Satan's lie — mankind lost a great deal. But the Bible says that what man lost through the first Adam, he has regained through the second Adam. Thus, the principle of spiritual authority continues to this day, restored and now present in the Body of Jesus Christ.

In Exodus 19:6, God said to Israel, *"And you shall be to Me a kingdom of priests and a holy nation...."* Notice that phrase "a kingdom of priests." God was signifying that His people are both kings *and* priests. This is confirmed in First Peter 2:5 and 9, where Christians are called "a holy priesthood" and "a royal (or kingly) priesthood."

God sent His Son Jesus to take the judgment of your sins upon Himself so you could become a citizen of Heaven and a kingly priest on this earth. *Rest assured — what happens to you matters greatly to God.*

# CHAPTER 20

I'll never forget that meeting. I had only been in the Redwood City board conference room twice before, both times in hypothetical discussions with no thought of establishing a continuing relationship. I was being sought after then, and they were the suitors. Now the atmosphere was changed — I could smell it in the air. An atmosphere of strained friendliness prevailed as the acting chairman cleared his throat.

"I'm afraid, Brother Howard, that we can't fulfill some of our promises."

My throat tightened.

"We've rechecked our resources, and it just isn't possible to extend the house loan. I'm sorry."

The acting chairman was referring to the board's agreement to help my family relocate into this far more expensive area by giving us an interest-free loan for a down payment on a house.

"And there is another matter," he said, speaking in his best authoritative manner with an underling. "We agreed to take over the payments on your Buick." He was referring to a lease car my brother-in-law had given me after my sister's death simply for continuing to make the monthly payments. "The budget won't allow that. Besides, a church member gave a station wagon to the church last year, and we believe that is good enough for business transportation."

I started to speak, but the man droned on as though I had already left the room. "Now, I realize that this alters our agreement, and if you wish to change your mind, we'll understand." Those last words were frightening and frigid. The room chilled as he spoke them.

I was angry and hurt. I felt like I'd been forced out on a limb, and it had been cut away. Just what was happening? What were the stakes? Anita's words replayed in my ears: "I don't trust them, Rick. It just isn't right."

I glanced around the room. These were good men — men who had invested their lives in church ministry. Something had happened for which they were unprepared, but something had also entered into their spirits.

"Gentlemen," I replied, "I told you that should you issue a call, it would simply lead me to begin a serious search for a word from God. I told you I couldn't be voted into this church — God would have to send me.

"Well, I know it is God's will for me to bring my family here and pastor this church, and I can't be frightened out of that fact now. I intend to begin immediately operating as chairman of this board and to begin my preparation for this ministry."

There was both relief and tension in the room. I knew I had faced a spirit I would face again. I also knew that God had sent me there. I silently prayed for strength and began my agenda with the board.

When we were finished, I walked alone to the large pastor's office behind the conference room. It was clean and bare with two orange conference chairs and a matching orange desk chair behind a huge, "L-shaped" desk. Homemade bookshelves lined every wall, empty except for some magazines and stacks of abandoned books on the lower shelves.

"Oh, God," I prayed, "I'm really not ready for this. I feel so alone and desperate. Can this be Your will? Have I heard amiss?" I bowed over the desk, flexing my fingers on the top. "Help me. Please help me."

I hadn't turned the lights on, and the office looked shadowy and enormously lonely. I turned and walked out into the reception area. One older member of the board was still standing there alone.

"Pastor," he said with tears in his eyes. "I'm glad you're staying with us." Then his voice broke. "I've never been through anything like this before; it's really been rough."

I reached out, and we hugged. It felt warm and good.

"We'll make it, Fred," I spoke. "We'll make it somehow as long as we can stay together."

"Yes," he smiled and chuckled. "*That's* the chore!"

And then we parted.

Driving over the San Mateo Bay Bridge was an experience that night. My heart was filled with strife and disappointment. I wondered what I should say to my wife, and my mind was filled with doubts about the entire situation. I turned on the radio; within a matter of minutes, the announcer spoke the name Redwood City twice. I didn't remember ever hearing that name before in the media.

I could hear Anita's words ringing in my ears — those infamous words she spoke on the telephone to me as I stood in the Sierras that day: "I have some bad news for you. Monday night they elected you to the Redwood City Church."

# Chapter 21

I told you earlier about a young surfer who was converted during my ministry at a church in North Hollywood, California. He had no church experience, and his conversion was opposed by his parents. I just handed him a Bible and said, "Start reading," without further instructions. I later found out that he started reading in the book of Genesis. That's certainly logical, since it's at the front of the Book, but Genesis is hardly the place for a young believer to start reading.

Nevertheless, this young man came back in mid-week and told me that he got so excited reading the Bible that he just had to go to the end to see how it all turned out. Then he said with a big smile, "Guess what? We win!"

That's not a bad way to begin one's understanding of the Word! In fact, this young believer's words encompass the essence of the Gospel. As Revelation 1:5 and 6 declares, *"...To Him* [Jesus Christ] *who loved us and washed us from our sins in His own blood, and has made us kings and priests to His God and Father, to Him be glory and dominion forever and ever. Amen."*

Again the book of Revelation adds, *"...For You were slain, and have redeemed us to God by Your blood out of every tribe and tongue and people and nation, and have made us kings and priests to our God; and we shall reign on the earth"* (Rev. 5:9,10).

I believe a divine call is going out to the Church world today that is just as sure as any prophetic call of God. God is calling believers to come out of Babylon and to begin understanding the uniqueness of His election and His call on their lives to be kings and priests unto Him in this day and generation.

However, as with the early Babylonian captives, most of us have our hands full of "building our own houses." Of course, this means more than simply constructing a building. It encompasses everything we build for ourselves in life — our security, our jobs, our families, our investments, our retirement.

That last issue is especially amazing among American Christians. We spend so much of our lives looking toward retirement. Even young men say, "Well, I have to put this away for my retirement. After all I want to retire when I'm still young." On the other hand, I often meet retired people who are bored to tears!

In fact, psychological studies have been conducted that suggest men often die in advance of medical causes because have they have been retired and have lost their sense of identity and purpose.

The call of God is always to move away from *only* building houses or establishing security systems. We must allow the Spirit of God to reveal to us who we really are.

You see, my friend, God has given *you* authority to pull down and root out. When He reveals that truth to you, something begins to happen in your heart.

Psalm 110 is the Old Testament prophecy that is most often repeated in the New Testament. You probably remember some of its phrases: *"The Lord said unto my Lord, Sit thou at my right hand, until I make thine enemies thy footstool"* (v. 1 *KJV*). That specific verse is quoted several times in the New Testament. It is of course referring to Jesus the Messiah. The Father is saying to His Son, "I have placed all Your enemies in subjection to You, even though this may not appear to be true when people reject and crucify You or when evaluating the fruit produced by Your Body through which I work."

But now look at the next verse, which is seldom quoted correctly: *"The Lord shall send the rod of thy strength out of Zion: rule thou in the midst of thine enemies"* (v. 2 KJV).

One doesn't have to be a profound Bible scholar to know that two principal symbols of authority are given in the Scriptures: the symbols of *gates* and of *the rod*. The rod of authority is the symbol of God's rule. But notice in this Psalm where it is located. The rod of His authority will come *out of Zion*.

Zion, of course, is always the place of assembly for God's people. To us today it means the Church. The writer to the Hebrews says, *"But you have come to Mount Zion and to the city of the living God, the heavenly Jerusalem, to an innumerable company of angels, to the general assembly and church of the firstborn who are registered in heaven..."* (Heb. 12:22,23).

Now what is being said? The Church of Jesus Christ is like a great colossus that has been pinned down to the sand of this earth by "Lilliputians" and their host of tiny, seemingly insignificant threads. Everyone wants to run up to the giant and say, "Get up! They're just threads — a bunch of nonessentials. Become the giant you were born to be!"

People often wonder why I have so little patience for the monotonous drivel of church experience. Should boys wear long hair? Is it all right to wear beards in church? Should we wear cuffs on our pants? Should we wear earrings? I'll tell you this: When this kind of drivel occupies the attention and energy of a local church, Satan is *delighted*.

So many of us spend the majority of our energy on totally nonessential things — on this club, that group, or this activity. Even the local church seems to be singing "Let Us Entertain You."

"We'll cook supper for your family on this night."

"We'll do this for your children and that for your grandmother."

What a loss of perspective of *our true destiny*!

Here is this colossus that has the rule of authority over the world — the Church of God that comes out of Zion — *wiping dishes*! Meanwhile, Satan laughs in derision at us. If only we had ears to hear God's message to us. No wonder Jesus so often said, "He who has ears to hear, let him hear."

At this point it's in my heart that we need to echo this prayer: Somehow, like Zechariah, may we learn to stand up and say, "The Lord showed me in His Word that He has raised me up to both pull down and establish kingdoms. The rod of God's authority is in the Church, and He has made me both a king and priest unto Him. My garments may be defiled from personal iniquity or by my representation of the sins of my people. Yet still I will come before God, for I have a ministry of intercession. I have a place before Him, and I will exercise my authority."

Without doubt, we are often in the role of Joshua in Zechariah 3. But unless we reach a place of personal identification, anything else we might learn about this passage will be weak and ineffective.

I believe God has some powerful, personal truths He wants to show us regarding this vision, but we must first personally identify with Joshua the high priest as he stands before God. This repetitive drama of history that went on then still goes on today! There is yet a work of restoration that needs to be done.

Spoken words have a very powerful influence in our lives, even when we are children. It's one of the things transactional analysis deals with in the world of psychology. When we were children, many of us heard a particular word spoken about us, and we have lived the rest of our lives proving that word to be true.

Maybe a young boy overhears a conversation between Mom and a teacher that goes something like this: "Well, you know, he fell on his head when he was three, and he's not all together there. He's a little slow in learning."

So that boy grows up and spends the rest of his life proving to the world that he is lacking something in the mental realm and that he really can't learn. He never stops to think whether or not it's true. He has just accepted that it must be true because someone said it.

Other people live out the expectation that they are ugly because a sister or brother called them ugly when they were children. Often these people never come to grips with the beauty that God has wrought in them. Others live out the spoken words, "He's very industrious," and they end up going to an early grave from trying so hard all their lives to *be* industrious.

The list goes on and on. I'm telling you, words are powerful things. No wonder Jesus said, *"For by your words you will be justified, and by your words you will be condemned"* (Matt. 12:37).

A young man who used to occasionally visit our assembly once spoke a word to me. I had utmost confidence in this young man, for I knew of no person in the entire church who spent as much time in prayer and intercession as he did. He was incredibly sensitive to the Holy Spirit — a wide-open, almost direct channel to God.

One Sunday night I continued to sit on the platform after the service was over. I was exhausted from the burden of the message I had just preached and even more exhausted from the thought of trying to see it become effective in people's lives. As I sat there, this young man approached me in a very unassuming manner and whispered in my ear, "Tonight while you were preaching, the Lord said to me..." Then he made a statement that, because of its private nature, I'll not quote. His words are less important than what happened to me after he spoke them. However, I will say that the essence of this young man's word from the Lord was along the line of "The Lord put the spirit of ___ in you this morning."

With that, the young man left. He didn't wait for me to say, "That could never happen" or "How could that be true?"

I went back to my office, and a drama began to unfold in my life over the course of the next week and a half. I began to experience a whole new sense of being, including a new sense of authority and of divine purpose.

A word had been spoken — a word that basically said, "Why are you living on this low level? Why are you concerned about the mundane? I've put you in a place of authority; I've put you in a position to rule. Why are you down here messing with trivial matters? I have a great purpose for you." It was as though someone had pulled the curtain back!

Now I want to suggest to you that the essence of what happened to me that night, the essence of the little drama that continued to unfold in my life from that moment forward, is reflective of what's going on in *you*.

The Holy Spirit would say to you, "You're a member of My Kingdom of priests; you are a ruler in this world. You are not the quirk of existential philosophy, tossed to and fro by the storms of this earth. You're supposed to *make* the waves, not ride under them. You're supposed to *change* kingdoms, not be affected by them. You are supposed to rule by the rod of authority, not react to what others' rules are saying. God has placed you in this position of authority."

Is it not possible that God is saying to us, "If you could only just understand what it is to stand before Me and intercede! Even with the unclean clothes of the Church, of this generation, and of yourself, keep on standing, for I have called you and elected you to stand with the authority and power that is granted to you on that basis." If we could only understand this vital truth!

An old chorus from my childhood echoes this responsibility:

Keep me true, Lord Jesus, keep me true.

There's a race that I must run,
There are victories to be won,
By Thy power every hour,
Keep me true.

The Bible relates what happened when God spoke to Daniel:

> **In the first year of his** [Darius'] **reign I, Daniel, understood by the books the number of the years specified by the word of the Lord through Jeremiah the prophet, that He would accomplish seventy years in the desolations of Jerusalem.**
>
> **Then I set my face toward the Lord God to make request by prayer and supplications, with fasting, sackcloth, and ashes.**
>
> Daniel 9:2,3

Daniel caught a glimpse and came to grips. He caught hold of the concept of who he was and what he could do!

So many of us are so concerned about nonessentials when God has called us to change and alter the course of history. We often think that the most significant thing we can do is to eat, drink, bear children, build houses, and go to work. Yet God has placed a rod of His divine authority in our hands, and He has said to us, "Govern, rule, and take authority."

It is everywhere as it was with Zechariah. The prophetic word always divides even the Church. In fact, it often divides God's people. As God raised up Zechariah with His vision, some people said, "Oh, no, we've heard this kind of thing before. We're going to keep building our own houses, planting our own trees, and raising our own vineyards." Surely many missed the moment of their destiny — an hour that God irreplaceably put in their hands.

People who "miss their moment" become a part of that indescribably innumerable army that marches through life in perpetual regret, saying, "If only I had listened, if only I had done, if only, if only, if only, if only..." First Corinthians 3:13-15 explains what will happen when these people stand before the Judgment Seat of Christ:

Each one's work will become clear; for the Day will declare it, because it will be revealed by fire; and the fire will test each one's work, of what sort it is.

If anyone's work which he has built on it endures, he will receive a reward.

If anyone's work is burned, he will suffer loss; but he himself will be saved, yet so as through fire.

Certainly many of the Christians standing at that moment will say, "If only, if only, if only. If only I had lifted my eyes beyond the trivial. If only I had known my eternal purpose in God through Christ. If only..."

That is the call that comes to us. However, I have no simplistic aspirations about changing the course of even a high percentage of people through preaching or writing.

A staff member once said to me, "It seems that preaching is an extremely ineffective method of spreading the Gospel."

I could only answer, "Yes. Isn't it strange that God has chosen it?"

Preaching is the weakest of all things I can imagine. Yet God has chosen the foolishness of preaching to save those who will believe in Christ. Throughout the eras of time, He has used the foolishness of proclamation and of prophecy to show the people who will truly hear how to alter their lives and thus change the course of history.

We must proclaim the Word of God without fear or failure. Our focus cannot be on searching for the best music or the most comfortable pews. It must not even be our purpose to search for the shortest service. A centered Christian must not respond to the "shotgun calls" of a passing culture.

God has put us on the line. We're on the target. We know what God has put us here to do, and we must do it as simply, yet as profoundly, as we know how to do it.

The prophetic word is the rock of offense and the stone of stumbling. Some will build their houses upon it, and upon others it will fall and grind them to powder.

May I end this chapter with a prayer for you?

Lord, You have chosen to work through the Church, although we don't understand why. You've chosen to work through us, and we can't understand that either! It seems impossible for our minds to comprehend.

Lord, Your Body in this day seems comprised of weakness. Even as Your apostle spoke, we seem to be the offscouring of the earth — the weak and despised. Among us there are not many mighty, nor are there many powerful after the flesh. Yet You chose us, Father. You've seen fit to put the rod of divine authority in the Church, which is us.

Lord, help us to somehow be convinced that we are indeed who You declare us to be, in spite of our failures and our limited works. Your faith in us has pronounced more than what our eyes have seen. Oh, Father, help us see it. Help us to begin acting like kings and priests on this earth — changing and revolutionizing the structure of the opportunity now set before us. Speak to us, we pray, in Jesus' Name. Amen.

# CHAPTER 22

I t was a long January night for Zechariah, the young Hebrew prophet. One after another, the successive revelations came, causing Zechariah to be numbered among the most complete prophets of all time. In one great panorama, Zechariah was taken from the Babylonian captivity and the restoration of the temple, which was the immediate context of his ministry, to the ultimate coming and eventual earthly reign of the Messiah. God was giving Zechariah the total revelation of Jesus.

But with all the drama and revelation spanning centuries of time, the key issue for Zechariah was his own context — the fifty thousand Jewish refuges who had returned from seventy years of Babylonian captivity. They had returned with high hopes and an earnest, fervent desire to rebuild the fallen temple of God. That temple was to be the very symbol of restoration.

As a nation, Israel was in fact built on the foundation of God's Presence. Therefore, the temple was the priority project. It represented the firstfruits of revival and characterized the firstfruits of a new personal and national life.

To us, the restoring of the temple is comparable to God's work in our lives through salvation and the baptism in the Holy Spirit. God is continually restoring unto us what the devil has stolen, causing us to become more effective witnesses at work and helping us get our families on a more solid Christian foundation. You see, restoration is always ultimately personal. That must constantly be our understanding.

Let us note again that restoration projects almost inevitably bring opposition from without. In this case, a mixed multitude of neighbors under Sanballat and Tobiah first laughed, then mocked, then discouraged, and finally persecuted the restorers as they attempted to sabotage the project.

But along with the outward opposition came the opposition of the complainers and the whiners from within. "This temple isn't nearly as nice as the last temple!" they cried. They literally wept in their dismay. Such encouragement!

What resulted from this outward and inward opposition? This sacred cause, this first purpose, this divine symbol of revival, renewal, and restoration came to a grinding halt.

Perhaps we should remember here what Jesus taught about a similar situation:

> "For which of you, intending to build a tower, does not sit down first and count the cost, whether he has enough to finish it —
>
> "lest, after he has laid the foundation, and is not able to finish, all who see it begin to mock him,
>
> "saying, 'This man began to build and was not able [the *Amplified* says, "not worth enough"] to finish.'"
>
> Luke 14:28-30

Jesus' words certainly apply to this specific instance. When these captivity restorers were brought to a halt for sixteen long years, the shadow of their incomplete temple became an object of mockery against the Lord.

How much like some of us! We've responded to Christ's call to begin again to be restored to God, to rebuild our lives, or to get our families in order. We start out to complete something God has told us to do, to "rebuild the temple" in our lives. Often we announce these high purposes to our families and friends. Our fellow workers and neighbors attentively watch. Sure, some criticize and some mock, but they all watch as we begin to build. Will we finish what we have started? Can we complete it?

More and more, I see that the real issue of this spiritual work stoppage is the one recorded in Zechariah 3. It is this fourth vision of Zechariah that I believe actually shows us the amazing reason God's work is not being done even today in so many people's lives.

As you remember, the vision concerns Joshua, the high priest of God. Zechariah is shown his young contemporary standing before the Lord. Although this Joshua is a direct descendent of Aaron the high priest, he is standing before the Lord in dirty robes. We have seen that the filthiness of Joshua's robes are representative of the sins of the people and of his own sins. Zechariah 3 further records that Satan stands at Joshua's right hand to be his adversary and to accuse him.

Joshua, of course, represents all of us as believers. We are kings and priests unto God. We share the throne of Christ; we rule by prayer. The Word of God reminds us in Psalms 110:2 that the Lord will send the rod of His strength out of Zion (a type of the Church) so He may rule in the midst of His enemies.

Derek Prince, previously quoted from his excellent book *Shaping History Through Prayer and Fasting*, writes, "All Christians look forward to the day when Christ's enemies shall have been finally and completely subdued, and He shall be openly manifested and universally acknowledged as king.

"The Bible promises this day will come, but we must not let the promised glory of the future blind us to the reality of Christ's present position at the right hand of God. Christ rules now in the midst of His enemies, and we rule with Him." He continues, "It is our responsibility to exercise the authority that is ours through His name, and in the face of all the forces of evil to demonstrate that Christ is already King of Kings and Lord of Lords."[11]

Oh, friend, how desperately we need to see this! In Zechariah 3, Joshua represents Israel brought to a standstill. The work to be done is left undone. The building to be built is unfinished. The testimony that would have been raised is instead a mockery.

How were God's people stopped? What brought such a cataclysmic failure to God's people after their purposes began so well? Was it the power of a conquering army? Of course not. Had any army raised its banner, the very armies of Heaven would have fought for Joshua and for Zerubbabel — indeed, for Israel.

Was it then a lack of funds? Of course not. The treasuries of Heaven and the total resources of this earth were being tapped by a sovereign God so this temple could be rebuilt. When you read the history, you find that even Cyrus, an ungodly king, was pouring monies from his own personal treasury into this restoration project in order to see the temple completed.

"Well, then, what?" you ask. "What could stop such a grand purpose? What could stop such an overwhelming project for God?"

Well, perhaps we should ask, "What stops *you* from being the person God intended you to be? What stops you from being God's priest? What stops you from building the temple God has told you to build? What stops you from shaping history through intercession?"

You see, this next step is so important, so simple, and yet so often missed. What is this second clear teaching from Zechariah's fourth vision? Simply, it is the nature of Satan himself — he whose

---

[11]Prince, op. cit., p. 36.

name is Diabolos, meaning *adversary*. He is the accuser, the chief of all slanderers, the clever father of lies, and the opposer of all good men and godly causes. Although his fate was written through the submission of Christ to the Cross and his eternal defeat is already assured, yet today he still pursues his goal of usurping authority.

You see, Satan rules only by our permission. His chief strategy must always be "the bluff"; his primary tools are fear and condemnation; and his only light is darkness. That is the chief point of Zechariah 3.

The account of Daniel's intercession in Daniel 9 and 10 also gives us insight into both the extent of our spiritual authority and the nature of our enemy. First, Daniel 9 relates the time the prophet Daniel received the revelation that Israel's time of captivity was almost over:

> **In the first year of his** [Darius'] **reign I, Daniel, understood by the books the number of the years specified by the word of the Lord through Jeremiah the prophet, that He would accomplish seventy years in the desolations of Jerusalem....**
>
> **Now while I was speaking, praying, and confessing my sin and the sin of my people Israel, and presenting my supplication before the Lord my God for the holy mountain of my God,**
>
> **yes, while I was speaking in prayer, the man Gabriel, whom I had seen in the vision at the beginning, being caused to fly swiftly, reached me about the time of the evening offering.**
>
> Daniel 9:2,20,21

Notice that when Daniel was given the prophetic view of what time it was on God's calendar, he set his face toward Heaven to not only confess his own sin, but also to representationally confess the sins of his people. This is exactly what Joshua was doing in Zechariah's vision. It is also what we as God's people can do for our nation in this hour.

Years later, after Daniel had spent three weeks in fasting and in intercession for his people, a Man appeared to him in a vision who appears to be the preincarnate Christ Himself, for He is described in the same manner as John's vision of Jesus Christ in Revelation 1:13-15:

> I lifted my eyes and looked, and behold, a certain man clothed in linen, whose waist was girded with gold of Uphaz!
>
> His body was like beryl, his face like the appearance of lightning, his eyes like torches of fire, his arms and feet like burnished bronze in color, and the sound of his words like the voice of a multitude.

> Daniel 10:5,6

What this Man said to Daniel is profoundly applicable to our present lives as believers:

> Then he said to me, "Do not fear, Daniel, for from the first day that you set your heart to understand, and to humble yourself before your God, your words were heard; and I have come because of your words.
>
> "But the prince of the kingdom of Persia withstood me twenty-one days; and behold, Michael, one of the chief princes, came to help me, for I had been left alone there with the kings of Persia.

> Daniel 10:12,13

What was the Man in the vision saying to Daniel? Who is the prince of the kingdom of Persia? Was this divine being, most likely the preincarnate Son Himself, stopped in His divine mission to bring a word from God to Daniel for twenty-one days by an earthly king? No, He was only delayed for a time. The prince of the kingdom of Persia was the demonic prince assigned to that particular natural kingdom. It was this demonic authority who delayed this Man of Daniel's vision from bringing the clear message to the prophet.

I believe that such dark princes are assigned not only to nations and peoples, but often to churches and to works of God all around the world as well. In this instance, even Daniel, a mighty man before God, is kept from an answer as a result of the intervention of Satan.

Now let's go back to Zechariah's vision of the high priest Joshua. In this passage of Scripture, Joshua was a man who, from the time he left Babylon, had set his heart to participate actively and sacrificially in the restoration of God's people. Like many of us, Joshua's heart was right and his purpose was clear. He knew it would cost something. He had left Babylon and come to see this work completed for God.

But Joshua wasn't a perfect man. He made a classic error when he allowed the descendants of God's people to intermarry with the heathen of the area. God had to judge that sin. Ezra later reveals the heartache and sorrow that resulted from reversing this devastating sin (*see* Ezra 10).

But here in Zechariah 3, we see Satan seeking to achieve the withdrawal of divine favor from Joshua because of his sin. Through this evil strategy, Satan was attempting to dispose of the entire covenant relationship of God's people.

What do you expect when you set your face to seek heartily after God? Do you expect your friends and neighbors or even Satan to applaud you? What do you really think will happen when you stand representationally before God on behalf of the nation in intercessory prayer? Do you think it will be as easy as eating ice cream or going to church? Of course not.

Joshua standing with dirty robes represents his own personal error and the sins of the people. Of course, Satan stands nearby to accuse. Nevertheless, God continually chooses Joshua, saying, "He's a brand plucked from the fire" (Zech. 3:2). It's as though the Father is saying, "I'm not going to put this half-burnt brand back into the fire again simply because all the evil hasn't been burned out of him. I have forgiven once; I will forgive again."

The army of God has often been debilitated without a single shot being fired. Jesus said about the Church, "...*The gates of hell shall not prevail against it*" (Matt. 16:18 *KJV*). The phrase "gates of hell" means *the authority or the power of hell.* Satan's power cannot prevail against the Church of Jesus Christ.

Then why in God's Name are we not overcoming Satan's strategies more often in this life? Why are our communities filled with violence and discrimination? Why do ultra-minorities govern our schools and political systems and thus determine what our children and our nation will be in the future? *Why are we not conquering?*

The apostle Paul wrote that we are to be engaged in *"casting down arguments and every high thing that exalts itself against the knowledge of God, bringing every thought into captivity to the obedience of Christ"* (2 Cor. 10:5). Why are these things not cast down in our lives? The Word says that we will rule as kings and priests. Why are we not ruling?

The answer is frighteningly simple, yet devastatingly effective. We are condemned. We are kept at the place of judgment — unworthy, stripped, guilty, and, worse yet, clothed in unrighteousness. Like Joshua, we stand with our head bent and hear the accusation of the enemy, over and over and over again. We are caught in a verbal tennis match. We've become debilitated by our conscience, and we've been made ineffective by our guilt. We're unable or unwilling to receive the Lord's verdict of forgiveness.

Listen, friend, Joshua the high priest can't in any way effectively intercede and mediate on behalf of God while he is in a place of accusation. Therefore, you can note this: Where he stands in the vision is *not* a place of judgment.

Satan cannot bring you to a place of judgment. He has no place to stand in God's literal time of judgment. Nevertheless, here he is, standing with the Lord and Joshua in Zechariah's vision. It seems the enemy is attempting an out-of-court settlement.

But in a sense, Satan has already won. Having succeeded in hauling Joshua into this place of accusation, Satan has already brought the work and progress of the restoration project to a stop. Joshua represents Israel, and he has been totally blocked.

This demonic strategy is often the enemy's best-kept secret. Satan uses feelings of inferiority to paralyze and immobilize us, and that's exactly what Zechariah 3 is about. Satan knows our flaws, and he moves in with such a cunning and deceptive glorification of them that he brings us to a standstill! All work stops; all advance for God's Kingdom stops; and we stand as did Joshua, with our heads bowed.

In this case, nothing more was done for sixteen years. Gradually, the work of restoration on the temple became a mere distant memory.

# CHAPTER 23

I think I developed relatively normally. One older church man told me at a poolside that I had a lot of hair on my legs, and I've already told you about my expanding hips. So the secondary sexual characteristics seemed to all be in place, and the primary area of interest seemed equally about on course. Comparisons generally eased my mind, although, admittedly, there had been some glances that had produced chagrin and concern on my part.

What's more, I liked girls, and there were a lot of them in my life — Carol, Sheleigh, Phyllis, Shirley, and Hazel — as well as a lot of growing and sincere friendships with other girls. Nothing truly sexual occurred in this arena with the exception of some adolescent experimentation, but I certainly had some big crushes — deep and painful commitments, often unrequited and obviously life-affecting. Through these growing-up years, I also had some meaningful, developing peer relationships with boys.

My parents' constant reminder, "Remember — you're not like other boys," was meant to be protective, but somehow it had a two-sided blade. Mom and Dad wanted my expectations to be realistic.

After all, an artificial eye was a handicap with both physical and social ramifications.

But how different was I? And what effect would it have on my future? These questions often haunted me.

Phyllis was a painful church affair. She was beautiful and, as is typical, two years ahead of my maturity level even though we shared the same birth year. She dazzled older boys as well. I was but a taga-long, good as an "in-between sport." But it didn't matter. The times Phyllis wore my ring or sat particularly close to me in church seemed wonderful and fanciful. I blamed my physical appearance for the on-and-off nature of our relationship, doubting my effective-ness as a man in spite of other girls who stood by and seemed inter-ested in me.

Then there was Donnie at youth camp. Donnie was an older boy, recently converted, and he became an immediate focus of my week. Although at the time I was dating Shirley, who was the most attractive girl at camp and had even caught Donnie's eye, it some-how wasn't enough. I desperately needed Donnie's acceptance, but, at best, he responded to me as a pesky little brother.

The source of Donnie's attitude toward me was my eye — I was sure of it. Photos of me during this time show me with a queer tilt of the head; I was growing more self-conscious daily.

Then there was the persistent rumor of miracles to deal with, along with the constant Pentecostal hype on divine healing. About this time, reports circulated that a young man was miraculously able to see through his "glass eye." Several times people wanted to exercise their "faith" on me. It was a private torture that has left me forever attentive to the plight of the handicapped or of those who are in some way different — particularly in this type of religious atmosphere.

It was during the aforementioned youth camp that I climbed the stairs to a chapel. Alone and desperate, doubtlessly pushed by my needs, I wrestled with God in my unique and individual agony.

"I know You can heal me, Lord," I prayed, "Give me a new eye. Let me see through this eye." I closed my good eye and squinted, imagining light pouring through the opaque darkness. I did other things that I felt were related to faith. But as is the case for many Christians, my faith was ultimately a form of *mere magic*, and the Father loved me too much to respond in kind.

However, as I prayed in desperation, I suddenly found that I was being answered. I was seeing, perhaps in a vision, a wandering little lamb. (Who can know for sure how their spiritual perceptions occur?) I knew this lamb. It was frivolous, always wandering away to seek different pastures, often falling over cliffs and getting caught in brambles. It seemed to be a personification. I recognized the spirit.

Then I watched as the Shepherd lovingly broke the lamb's leg. At first, this act seemed cruel and heartless. But then He carefully set the limb and bandaged the break.

What occurred next in my sight was almost indescribable. The Shepherd carried the lamb constantly in the crook of His arm. In the wonder of vision, I somehow knew that many days had passed for the lamb and Shepherd.

When the Shepherd finally set the formerly wayward lamb down, I watched as the little lamb followed close and fast to the Shepherd. It had been an important process, one that had been based on foreknowledge and loving, purposeful discipline.

No one had ever told me that story; it would have been presumptuous if they had. But in the spirit of the Holy Place, my vision proved to be a clearer answer for me than a spoken word. That answer didn't clear away the pain, fear, or frustration. But it brightened an understanding; it revealed a purpose; and it deepened a growing sense of self-understanding.

Prone to wander, Lord, I feel it,
Prone to leave the God I love;

Here's my heart, O, take and seal it;
Seal it for Thy courts above.[12]

---

[12]"Come, Thou Fount of Every Blessing." Words by Robert Robinson, 1758.

# CHAPTER 24

Several years ago at the church I pastored for thirty years, Hal Lindsay, the author of *The Late Great Planet Earth,* was a guest speaker. We had dinner that evening before he spoke, and he told me about a manuscript he was working on at that time. He described devastating experiences he had gone through while working on this particular book. He said, "I think I'm going to call it *Satan Is Alive and Well on Planet Earth.*"

Hal then went on to describe how the enemy's strategies had also been clearly directed against the families of his staff members and his researcher. In the course of writing the book, Hal had even reevaluated some aspects of his theology as he became more aware of the supernatural in this era of Church history.

Shortly after Hal was with us, I received a copy of the new manuscript. I read it in one setting on a flight back to Wisconsin. Immediately I wrote Hal a letter, first congratulating him on the book and then disagreeing on a couple points. But what is important for this discussion is the last paragraph of my letter. I wrote, "Hal, the most important chapter of that book will not be read by most of the people who need it. I suggest that you print that chapter as a separate pamphlet or booklet."

Hal subsequently wrote a very kind letter acknowledging my letter and telling me that he was going to print the chapter I had mentioned in a separate booklet called *The Guilt Trip*. When you open that little book, you find this incredible statement:

> If you were the captain of an invading army, you'd find the weakest spot in your opponent's defenses, and then you'd go in for the kill. Satan, the archenemy of the saints, has a way of wiping out Christians over and over again. He moves in on our blind side and steers us in the direction he wants. When a person becomes a true believer in Christ, he is born into the family of God, and out of the family of Satan. And each time someone responds to the gospel, it's a slap in Satan's face. C. S. Lewis, in his amusing book, *The Screwtape Letters,* satirizes the daily routine in hell, and the foibles and headaches of hard working demons who just try to put in an honest day's work, fouling up Christians. And he then concludes, "The most successful tactics the demons use to neutralize their enemies, the Christians, was to get them to dwell on their failures. Once they began feeling guilty about their performance and the Christian life, they were no longer any threat to Satan's program." Things haven't changed much in Satan's tactics. Why should they? He's got a winner. There is nothing Satan likes better than to get a believer started on the guilt trip.[13]

Dr. James Dobson, formerly an eminent professor of pediatrics at USC School of Medicine and the president of the Behavioral Research Section of Children's Hospital in Los Angeles and now a leading Christian activist, once listed six psychological warfare tools he believes Satan uses against believers. These tools are incredible and revealing. They have so much to say about the enemy's warfare against us.

---

[13]Hal Lindsey, *The Guilt Trip* (Uhrichsville, Ohio: Barbour Publishing, Inc., 1996).

You see, Satan is not a mythological figure with a red suit and long tail. He is a dangerous adversary who has in his possession a powerful arsenal of weapons to use against us. His greatest weapon is that he knows our weaknesses and flaws and he knows how to use those weaknesses and flaws to his greatest advantage. Disappointments, disillusionment, failures — all these are things that often cause the Christian to abandon his position of faith.

In Ruth Paxson's amazing commentary on the book of Ephesians, she writes that Satan can only do three things to a Christian. First, he can despoil the Christian of his wealth. In other words, he can cause the Christian not to know what his wealth is in Christ, to take away his inheritance. Second, he can decoy the Christian from his walk. And third, he can disable the Christian from his warfare.[14]

The six psychological tools that Dr. Dobson lists are as follows:

1. *Fear and anxiety:* It wasn't for nothing that Jesus said, "Two things will prevent most of you from entering the Kingdom: the cares of this life and the deceitfulness of riches." Fear and anxiety are tremendous tools of discouragement in the lives of so many people.

2. *Guilt:* This second tool is referring to the kind of guilt that defies God's forgiveness and continues to torment you even after you've confessed your sin to the Lord. This guilt is not from God; rather, it comes from Satan in the form of condemnation and becomes the kind of guilt that seems unforgivable.

3. *Doubt and pessimism:* This is the third psychological tool Satan uses so effectively. Satanic in its origin and debilitating in its effect, doubt and pessimism destroys purposeful life.

4. *Anger and hostility:* Satan's fourth psychological tool of anger and hostility grows out of the frustrations that are caused by the difficulties in our lives.

---

[14]Ruth Paxson, *The Wealth, Walk and Warfare of the Christian* (New York: Revell, 1939).

5. *Fatigue:* According to Dr. Dobson, the fifth tool in the enemy's psychological warfare against the believer is fatigue. A person is never more open and vulnerable to Satan's destructive ideas than when his body is physically drained of energy.

   Vince Lombardi, a former coach of the Green Bay Packers and an inimitable leader of men, was known to frequently say, "Fatigue make cowards of us all." Jesus Himself said to His disciples, "Come apart and rest." Fatigue is indeed an effective psychological tool that the enemy uses against the believer.

6. *Inferiority and inadequacy:* This sixth tool that James Dobson gives is the one we see in Zechariah 3. The widespread, deep-seated feeling of inferiority and inadequacy is perhaps the most effective tool in the enemy's arsenal, head and shoulders above every other tool he uses. This tool includes the nagging self-doubts and the bitter disappointments of "who I am" or "what I have become."

I believe the context of Zechariah 3 makes it clear that this sixth tool of the enemy was a large part of Joshua's problem. Personally, he had made some serious blunders, especially in allowing the people to intermarry with the people of the land. He also represented the sins of his people, the returning refugees. Both he and they had been captives. They had been beaten; they had been defeated; they were ready at any moment to believe whatever lie was said by anyone about themselves. Such a yielding to the enemy in this area of inferiority is often the best-kept secret of the year among the people of God.

Satan uses these feelings of inferiority to paralyze us and to immobilize us, and that's exactly what Zechariah 3 is about. Satan knows our flaws, and he moves in with such incredibly cunning deception. He glorifies our flaws, and he brings us to a standstill. All work stops. All advance for God stops. We stand, as did Joshua, with our heads bowed. And as we have seen, in Joshua's case nothing was done for sixteen years to further the purpose of restoration.

# CHAPTER 25

W e have looked at the six psychological tools Satan uses against restorers, named by the famous psychologist and Christian activist, Dr. James Dobson. Once when Dr. Dobson spoke at our church, he told the story of a young junior high student named Danny. This young man was overweight, struggling with acne, and possessed an incredibly low level of self-esteem. The young man's problems were too long unidentified by those who might have been able to help him. Ultimately, he took his own life on his school campus.

Sometime after Danny's death, Dr. Dobson told his story to an audience at one of America's largest theological institutions. Later that same night, he received a letter where he was staying from one of the seminary students.

This is what the student had written:

Dear Dr. Dobson, I am one of the "Dannys" you spoke about in chapel today. Believe me, I've experienced this for as long as I can remember. It is a miserable way to live. Yes, I am a student at this seminary, but that doesn't make the problem any less acute. Through the years, particularly the last five, I have periodically gained a revived hope that somehow this problem can be overcome. Then to my great disappointment, I find that it is still very much a part of me. That's when I lose hope of ever conquering it. I want to be a minister of the Gospel, and I feel that this is God's will. *At the same time, I am aware of the paralyzing effect that this problem has on me.*

You see, Satan always takes the flaw and magnifies it.

Since the above letter was unsigned, Dr. Dobson read it in chapel the next day. At the end of chapel, many people came to thank the speaker. Meanwhile, the young man who had written the letter stood back and waited at the very end of the line. As the president of the seminary stood waiting for Dr. Dobson to finish with the students, he saw this young man talking to Dr. Dobson and "put two and two together." Later at lunch, the president said to Dr. Dobson, "Of all the young men in this seminary, that student would have been the last one I ever would have expected to suffer from feelings of inadequacy or inferiority." The president just couldn't believe it!

In relating this story, Dr. Dobson told me, "Rick, there was another young man in that service. I don't know where he was sitting; I never saw him, but he was there. The reason I know this is that three weeks after I left that seminary, I received a call from one of his roommates. Five young men had rented a house near campus and were living together as roommates. This roommate called me, shocked and shaken, to tell me that this other young man, this seminary student, had hung himself to death in the basement of their house. Even more amazing is that the others were so unaware of their roommate's problems, his body had gone undiscovered for five days!"

You see, the demonic tool of inferiority and inadequacy is the best-kept secret of the year! Believers who have yielded to the devil's torment in this area constantly struggle to keep their heads above water. It isn't a matter of being effective; it's a matter of *surviving* under the debilitating introspection that Satan brings to keep believers from experiencing true restoration.

This kind of personal debilitation is often our excuse to explain why we don't do the work of God. As a pastor, it's the most frustrating thing in the world. For every nine or ten people I ask to do a work, there is only one who will accept the job. The excuses are like the sundry rays of the sun:

- "I can't teach."
- "I'm not good before people."
- "I don't meet people well."
- "I don't do well with that kind of worship music."
- "I don't respond well to people in that situation."
- "I haven't sung a special for fifty years."
- I have never tried that."

Perhaps we need to read Exodus 3 and 4 carefully. When God calls Moses to lead His people out of Egypt, Moses begins by saying, "They won't even know who I am if You send me to them" (Exod. 3:11). Then Moses says, "And even if You did send me to my people, they would say, 'How do we know God has sent you? God didn't send you. You didn't have a revelation of God'" (Exod. 4:1).

Even after God takes care of that problem, Moses comes back again and says, "Well, there's something else I haven't told you, Lord. I better tell You this too. I stutter; I don't speak very well; and I'm not really very 'together.' The truth is, Lord, I just wouldn't be very effective" (Exod. 4:10). So God handles that problem as well.

Finally, Moses comes back in verse 13 and says, "Oh, God, I pray You'll send someone else. Can't You find someone else to send?"

Perhaps we should all underline verse 14 (*NAS*), which says, *"Then the anger of the Lord burned against Moses...."*

Hey, friend, God doesn't choose superstars to do His work. If you study the Scriptures from Genesis to Revelation, you'll find that He chooses people who have flaws and shortcomings — the Rahabs, the Gideons, the Davids, and on down the line. They are all flawed people who have many shortcomings but who at least allow God to work through them.

I must also say that Satan uses these feelings of inferiority to contaminate our relationship with God. It amazes me (and it may surprise you as well) that there are Christians who are actually mad at God!

Why shouldn't they be angry with God? If they feel that they are worthless, inevitably they have to feel that the One who designed them had something against them when it all started out. Surely, He couldn't love them very much. After all, it's His fault they are the way they are. They don't really count for anything.

A young boy named Chris wrote his child psychotherapist, "Dear Dr. Gardner, What is bothering me is that long ago, some big person, a boy about thirteen years old, called me a turtle, and I know he said that because of my plastic surgery. I think God hates me because of my lip, and when I die, He'll probably send me to hell. Love, Chris."

It's pretty hard to get into what that little lad was feeling. It was all wrapped up in his belief that the kind of rejection he had known from people was what he'd get when he stood before God. He believed that one day, he'd knock on the doors of Heaven, and God would say, "I don't want you here." Believe me, Satan uses feelings of inferiority in an effort to contaminate the believer's relationship with God!

Losing my left eye when I was barely three years of age left me open to feeling bitterness as a young man. It was often an absolute quandary. I wanted to love God with one part of my heart, and I wanted to be angry with Him with another part. Just as the men of the Old Testament did, I wanted to ask, "Why did You make me thus? Why, *why*?"

Of course, this way of thinking originates in a lie of the enemy. This lie is based on a false introspection — a sense of inferiority that comes as a flaw and is played upon by Satan. But all too often we accept the lie and become debilitated. We stand with our hands folded, ineffective and immobile.

Satan also uses inferiority to impose conformity on us and on our children. Perhaps the greatest example is with teenagers. Suppose five young people are riding in a car and four of them start passing a drug. The fifth one knows in his mind that this isn't right. In his spirit, he knows it is not pleasing to God. But because of his feelings of inadequacy, he is unable to take a stand. Thus, he goes along with the other four. In other words, he chooses to conform.

There was a humorous and yet revealing story told in the Los Angeles press several years ago about a teenage choir that was performing on the stage of a great auditorium. They were singing "The Battle Hymn of the Republic" before an audience of teachers. Everyone knows how emotional that song is. These young people were getting into it, "glory hallelujahing" like mad. Suddenly, one of the young ladies on the front row got so caught up and excited that she passed out.

Like a fever in forty-eight impressionable minds, the idea of passing out became the accepted thing to do; nevertheless, the young people went on singing. Suddenly, *boom,* one collapsed on the back risers; *boom,* another fell in the middle; *boom,* one went down on the left; *boom,* another went down on the right. By the time the choir had reached the final "His truth is marching on," twenty-four bodies lay on the stage!

I have news for you. Satan's use of this effective tool of inferiority is causing many Christians to conform rather than to concentrate on becoming who God intends for them to be in this day. This problem isn't just with forty-eight emotional teenagers; it is rampant in the Church of Jesus Christ as a whole. Too many of us are asleep and lethargic while our temple remains unbuilt. The nation is being delivered into the hands of a minority because, unfortunately, we really don't know who we are.

I must also say that Satan uses this sense of inferiority to isolate us from other people. This may be his greatest weapon.

I see this problem so much in the Church. We pull within ourselves. We withdraw and take no risks. We pull back the curtains and peer at the world through our window as it passes by. We hold back from committing ourselves to social involvements. We pretend excessive meekness. As one comic has said, "The meek shall inherit the earth because they'll be too timid to refuse it!"

This is the way so many Christians live — isolated, ineffective, and withdrawn. People whom God meant to be beautiful and strong become defeated victims of satanic isolation.

The Beatles often wrote songs that were piercing social commentaries. One of their most biting commentaries was a song about the Anglican Church called "Eleanor Rigby." The theme person was an isolated, single person who went to church but was never known.

> Ah, look at all the lonely people.
> Eleanor Rigby
> Picks up the rice in the church
>     where a wedding has been
> Lives in a dream
> Waits at the window,
> Wearing a face that she keeps in the jar
>     by the door
> Who is it for?
> All the lonely people,
> Where do they all come from?
> All the lonely people
> Where do they all belong?

Not be outdone, the Beatles then take on the ministry:

Father McKenzie,
Writing the words of a sermon no one will hear
No one comes near
Look at him working,
Darning his socks in the night
    when there's nobody there
What does he care?
All the lonely people
Where do they all come from?
All the lonely people
Where do they all belong?

When the final verse arrives, you have almost anticipated the conclusion:

Eleanor Rigby
Died in the church and was buried along with her name
Nobody came
Father McKenzie
Wiping the dirt from his hand as he walks
    from the grave
No one was saved
All the lonely people
Where do they all come from?
All the lonely people
Where do they all belong?
Ah, look at all the lonely people. [15]

To be honest, Eleanor Rigby lives on my street. She sits in the pews of our churches — along with her masculine counterpart, of course.

---

[15]From the movie "*Yellow Submarine.*" Performed by the Beatles. Written by John Lennon and Paul McCartney, 1966.

James Dobson also describes a phone call he received one afternoon from a lady who attended his evangelical church. She had gone to that church as long as he had, somewhere between eight to twelve years. Dr. Dobson admitted he hadn't even known she was there.

The woman was middle-aged and had never been married. When she came to Dr. Dobson's office and started talking about her loneliness, it was obvious she hadn't come to obtain sympathy; she had just come to express the emptiness. "I have nobody," she told him. "Life gets pretty lonesome."

Dr. Dobson responded, "You really need a friend, don't you?"

A tear trickled down the woman's cheek, and she reached in her purse to take out a note she had written for herself at midnight one night. She hadn't intended for Dr. Dobson to read it. He read these words:

> Do you know how it feels to be blue?
> Do you know what it's like to feel
> nobody cares how things are with you?
> Yes, it's nice to be friendly at church time; you're thankful
> when they tell you they pray.
> But what about long, lonely night hours,
> not to mention the following day?
> You can call up your friends, and I do that;
> you can ask them how they are too.
> But you wished that they'd say,
> "Come over and help us eat up the leftover stew."
> Most everybody has a son or a daughter,
> a husband, a mother, or sis.
> But when you're alone with no loved ones,
> to me I just merely exist.

The nationally known psychologist added, "I looked right past that woman to my friends on the other side of the church for years and never saw she was there."

What a good job Satan has done. How neatly he has used the basic flaws and inferiority feelings we possess (and there are only a few of us who don't) to cause us to stand, as Joshua did in Zechariah 3, with head bent — aware of our weaknesses, introspective about our needs, completely immobilized and debilitated.

In this sad state, we are saved but useless. Who has the key? Who can change it?

# CHAPTER 26

W e have already traced God's identity with restorers and, through the Joshua vision, God's response to Satan in defense of the restorer's weakness and sin. We must all ultimately and decisively stand in the clarity of God's purpose.

> **And the Lord said to Satan, "The Lord rebuke** [and continue to rebuke] **you, Satan! The Lord who has chosen** [and continues to choose] **Jerusalem rebuke you! Is this not a brand plucked from the fire?"**
>
> Zechariah 3:2

Please notice that the Lord's defense of His choice comes before the descriptive phrase of Joshua's — and, thus, Israel's — condition.

> **Now Joshua was clothed with filthy** [literally "excrement-bespattered"] **garments, and was standing before the Angel** [called "the Lord" in verse 2].
>
> Zechariah 3:3

It is personal, not presumptuous, to see ourselves in these verses. Those of us who are called to restoration can in the process become wearied, disengaged, and even resentful, sullen, and disobedient.

Our garments can also become stained, even though we are thoroughly aware of the need for purity.

I believe you miss the point of this story — this vision in the night — unless you understand what this scenario of Joshua standing before the Lord and Satan standing at Joshua's right hand to oppose him represents: sixteen long years of a delayed project — of paralyzing immobilization and deferred authority. Zechariah sees Joshua standing there, debilitated, immobile, unable to do what God has called him to do. The prophet also sees Satan attacking Joshua with his accusations, producing a tug of war that seems impossible to resolve.

Finally the Lord orders Joshua's filthy garments to be replaced.

> **Then He** [the Lord] **answered and spoke to those who stood before Him, saying, "Take away the filthy** [excrement-bespattered] **garments from him** [Joshua].**" And to him He said, "See, I have removed your iniquity from you, and I will clothe you with rich robes."**
>
> Zechariah 3:4

Now, when you read this sequence consecutively in Zechariah, it seems quickly resolved. "What's the big deal?" you may ask. However, you must see the vision in the context of what actually happened. As you do, you will automatically ask, "Why did God take sixteen long years to end this immobilizing accusation? Why did He take sixteen years to affirm His choice of Jerusalem (Joshua and the restorers) in spite of their debilitating failure and sin?"

Since this book has been both a devotional exposition of the book of Zechariah (chapters 1-4) and a candid series of personal snapshots from my life, let me tell you of my first emotional identification with Zechariah's fourth vision and Joshua's dilemma.

My early years at Redwood City were often devastating, in spite of marked blessing and obvious signs of restoration. I took the battles very personally and often perceived confusion and disillusionment among others as personal attacks. My "life-phasing" was out of order. There were few times of "coming apart to rest awhile" and more times of simply coming apart! However, I continued to be upbeat, visionary, and courageous, recognizing some obvious signs of God's anointing and blessing.

But when I was alone, I would often just want to withdraw, feeling wounded and at times despondent. At one of my lowest moments, my wife, always supportive and highly perceptive, said to me, "Rick, you need to go somewhere alone and recover your objectivity." In a sense, she patted me on the fanny and said, "Go get better!"

I traveled south in California to a favorite hideaway that has small cottages built on a pier and actually hovers over a section of the beach and ocean. The travel had taken a day. I arrived late at night and got into bed without unpacking.

When I awoke and unpacked, I became aware that I hadn't even brought my Bible. So much for spirituality!

Nevertheless, on the coffee table of the small living area of the cottage was an old, black Bible. (The Gideons will get you every time!) I picked it up more out of religiosity than faith, and it fell open to Zechariah 3. (Do you doubt such "coincidences"?) I had read and studied this passage before, but on this particular morning it was painfully personal.

I was standing before the Lord in filthy garments. I was hearing His deliberate choice in spite of failure, and His awareness of the "brand-plucked-from-the-fire" nature of my incompletion and failure. I heard Him order the filthy robes stripped away; then He ordered rich robes to be brought to cover my nakedness.

Suddenly I was aware more deeply than ever of the story's context, and I heard my voice speaking almost in accusation, "Why did You wait sixteen years to tell Joshua this? How unfair that it took that long to resolve his turmoil!"

Now, I'm not given to visions or voices. My experience with direct "words from the Lord" is very limited. But I heard clearly that particular morning — clearly concerning Joshua and clearly concerning myself:

"Son, I didn't wait sixteen years to tell him. *He* waited sixteen years to hear *Me!*"

# CHAPTER 27

It will seem irrational to some that I choose to end this little devotional with an interruption. For an author to choose such a strategy could be interpreted as dysfunctional and incomplete. However, from the perspective of restoring restorers, I believe a discussion on Zechariah's interruption to be most accurate and well-placed.

Let me repeat the Lord's climatic word to young Joshua the high priest, as heard and seen by Joshua's contemporary, Zechariah.

> Then He answered and spoke to those who stood before Him, saying, "Take away the filthy garments from him." And to him He said, "See, I have removed your iniquity from you, and I will clothe you with rich robes."
>
> Zechariah 3:4

How do you think Zechariah received this vision? Was it shown on the ceiling of his bedroom (remember, it was a January night) in a sort of pre-IMAX "you-were-there" film? Or did the characters appear standing at the end of Zechariah's bed in some kind of "ahead-of-its-time" hologram?

All such questions are wasted speculation. Nevertheless, the next verse is a real shocker. When young Zechariah hears the words and sees the Lord's act of restoration on behalf of this biblical restorer named Joshua, he does the impossible: He jumps into the middle of his own vision!

How does one do that? It would seem akin to suddenly entering a projected movie and interacting with the characters!

> **And I** [Zechariah] **said, "Let them put a clean turban on his head." So they put a clean turban on his head, and they put the clothes on him. And the Angel of the Lord** [the Lord Himself] **stood by.**
>
> **Zechariah 3:5**

What does that mean? What is Zechariah doing in his own vision? What's he doing up on the stage?

The "turban" was the final piece the priest put on and the ultimate expression of confirmation regarding who he was. It was a miter, the last and most affirming thing done to say, "You really are who God wants you to be."

By jumping in with his own suggestion, Zechariah affirmed that he believed in this priest, regardless of his personal failure. It's as though Zechariah was saying, "Complete the process; put the turban on his head. He deserves it; that's who he is. He belongs to the family of God, regardless of the failures and inadequacies. All that God has rests in him, so put the turban on his head."

This scenario — this interruption — is classically important in restoring restorers. God has acted to end Joshua's dilemma, but, in truth, someone else is always needed to cancel Satan's accusations and get the restorer back to his foundations. A contemporary is needed — someone to throw his arms around the restorer in his night of personal loneliness and failure or in the hell of depression. That fact alone provides a clear basis for using this subject as a conclusion to our parable.

A priest has three basic functions, and all believers find their purpose in this priestly description. First, his task is to obtain unlimited access to God Himself by receiving Jesus as his Savior and Lord. Second, his task is to bring other people to God. Third, it is his responsibility to make offerings (or intercessions) to God on behalf of himself and others.

But perhaps the most significant thing I can say about the priesthood is that the Latin word for "priest" is "pontifex," which actually means *a bridge-builder*. The "pont" (as in "pontoon") is the bridge, and the priest is the bridge-builder.

There are so many people in God's world, and each one is a unique gift of God's heavenly creation. Every person first born of man and then born again of the Spirit is in truth a unique dream or vision of God. Paul writes to the Philippians that when God stops us in the process of our lives and chooses us, He apprehends us with a special job for us to do. We are apprehended for a purpose in Christ Jesus (Phil. 3:12). Yet so many of us, having been born again, could ask the question, "Is there life after rebirth?"

You see, the question that permeates today's society isn't "Is there life after death?" That question is hardly being asked. The question today that dominates people's minds is this: "Is there any purpose after you're born? Is there any life after birth?

For many Christians, it's the same thing. They get born again; they are responsive to God. Then somehow they become debilitated. Attacked by Satan, they start feeling guilty, inadequate, and condemned. They stand with head bowed, immobile and unable to finish the task God has called them to do.

We must learn this truth: Christians have the keys to self-esteem for the Joshuas of this world.

I don't know how long it was before I discovered that self-esteem doesn't come from achievement. A person can have his wall lined with his achievements, but that won't change his self-esteem.

Self-esteem doesn't come from materialism, nor does it come from race. Self-esteem comes but one way to a person — through human acceptance. It comes no other way. A person's self-esteem can only come through the channel of human acceptance, bestowed on him by giving, caring people.

In Matthew 25, Jesus talks about Judgment Day, when He tells the righteous, *"For I was hungry and you gave Me food; I was thirsty and you gave Me drink; I was a stranger and you took Me in"* (v. 35).

The righteous immediately ask, "When, Lord? Sure, we would have fed You when You were hungry, but we never saw You hungry. When did You come to us thirsty? When did You beg us to come to You in prison, or when were You naked?"

Jesus replies, "In that you've done it to the least of these, you've done it unto Me" (Matt. 25:40).

Why does Jesus say that? Because we have the keys that can totally break Satan's bonds of inferiority in believers' lives.

Imagine that, instead of Zechariah, *you* were given a vision in the night concerning a specific spiritual leader in your own circumstances. You see this leader standing with head down, subjected to accusation, and what's more, clothed in unrighteousness. He stands in smelly, obscene garments before our Lord. Would you celebrate this leader's restoration? Would you rejoice in the Lord's rebuke to Satan: "The Lord rebuke you and continue to rebuke you, Satan"? Would you joy in hearing the Lord say, "I have chosen and continue to choose this man. I knew thoroughly where he was when I found him; I chose him and plucked him as brand out of the fire"?

You see, I believe that, like Zechariah, we can jump into the middle of our knowledge and defend people who are immobilized and debilitated. Certainly there are many of them out there.

When I look at an average congregation of Christians, I think, *If we could harness these people, we could conquer the world.* Yet I know many of these Christians stand with head bent — debilitated, under attack, feeling inferior, tossed by the waves of everything Satan brings to them. And they've been there for years!

Some started to teach a class, and someone criticized them. That was twenty years ago, and it brought their ministry to a close. Some sang in the choir, and somebody critiqued their voice negatively. That was fifteen years ago, and they've never gone back into ministry. Perhaps they went door to door witnessing, and someone rebuked them. They've never done it again. Or maybe they started entering into praise, and their very family made fun of them. Since then, they have never opened their hearts to God in a time of worship.

In essence, all these people were taking a step to "rebuild the temple" in one way or another. But a negative word was spoken, followed by feelings of inadequacy. This satanic attack, whether through humans or otherwise, caused them to stop the progress on the restoration of their lives. So many will stand at the Judgment Seat of Christ with nothing in their hands because of this very scenario.

I have seen a little slogan printed on some calendars. It is anonymous but contains an incredible word: "Someday after we've mastered the winds and the waves, the tides and gravity, we will learn to harness for God the energies of love, and then for the second time in the history of the world, man will have discovered fire. The fire for God, and the adequacy for man."

I am absolutely convinced that Zechariah 3 and the story of Joshua is exactly why the Church is often immobile today. As the accuser and adversary, Satan has taken the flaws and inabilities of our human character and magnified them until we have come to a grinding halt. Many Christians can't even hear the verdict of the Lord, which says, *"Forgiven; chosen."*

Someone standing in the role of "priest" must somehow come with the key of self-esteem and unlock the bondage of these Christians. They must hear a contemporary proclaim, "Put a turban on his head. He really is a priest" or "She really is what God wants her to be. She is beautiful; she is usable; she is a handmaiden of the Lord." Someone must say, "Put turbans on their heads," so they can go forth to do what this passage says next: rule the house of God; have access to His courts; and be given a place to stand in His Presence.

> **"Thus says the Lord of hosts, 'If you will walk in My ways, and if you will perform My service, then you will also govern My house and also have charge of My courts, and I will grant you free access among these who are standing here.**
>
> **Zechariah 3:7 *NAS***

How long will we believe a lie? How long will we act out a deceptive fantasy, brought by the enemy of our soul to keep us ineffective? How long will the memory of failure and the guilt of sin destroy our standing before Christ? How long will we be ineffective in the place God has for us because we believe the debilitating lie of the enemy about our inferiority and inadequacy? When will we stand on His promise and claim the rights and privileges of sonship and daughterhood?

Satan is terrified over what would happen if even ten percent of Christians would turn from his lie and begin to exercise their authority in Christ. The Church would blow the enemy's ramparts off the territory of its vision! Christians would indeed conquer kingdoms and pull down strongholds. What's more, they would enjoy a loving fellowship in which human beings are continually affirmed. There would be no more Eleanor Rigbys in the Church!

I was once reading the apostle Paul's description of a loyal, sacrificial friend. He described this person as someone who "refreshed" him, or as the *Living Bible* describes it, as one whose visits were "like a breath of fresh air"[16] (2 Tim. 1:16). This friend sought Paul out during a time when any association with him was dangerous from

---

[16] *The Living Bible: Paraphrased* (Wheaton, Illinois: Tyndale House Publishers, 1971), p. 969.

the viewpoint of the government. The friend was not ashamed of Paul's "chains," and he ministered to him.

When I came to understand the depth of this description, the intensity and sacrifice of this relationship, I cried out to God: "Oh, how I long for such a friend!" Deep in my spirit, I heard these words: *"Become such a friend."*

# Chapter 28

If you've been sidelined, it isn't God who did it. He doesn't have a second team. God doesn't "red-shirt." Every person who is on the team of the Father has a job. So if you're "red-shirted," it's the enemy or yourself who has done it.

If you think you're "second team" and you're waiting for some new word of revelation, it will never come! God has given you a job, so get on with it — do it!

Some of us think our place on God's team is an issue of age. I'll tell you, I get so disturbed with this culture's preoccupation with youth. So many folks are involved in this effort to look and act and talk like young people! I don't know about you, but when someone says to me, "Oh, if only I could be young again," my immediate response is "God, help me never again to be a teenager!"

To me, it would be the greatest curse of eternity for God to say, "You're going to be an adolescent again for ten years." I think I'd respond, "Oh, Lord, anything but that!"

People are constantly wrestling with a desire to go back to some forgotten era. That's one big reason the Church of Jesus Christ gets sidelined like a train that's been pulled off the coupling to a side-track; meanwhile, the secular culture rolls on.

Many of us sit around, letting ourselves be sidetracked for years on end because we think it's too late. "God called me to go to Bible college when I was twenty and I didn't go," we say, "so I've been sidetracked ever since."

Who told you that you were sidetracked?

"God wanted me to be a missionary to Africa, but I married John, so I've missed the will of God for my life."

Who told you God had *only one unchangeable plan* for your life?

At sixty-five, Dr. Lillian Martin was forced to retire from Stanford University. The day she took her last salary check, she opened a child guidance clinic in Palo Alto, California. Later she opened a senior center to help older people find their abilities and potentials. At seventy-six, she learned to drive a car for the first time and promptly drove back and forth across the United States six times. At seventy-nine, she made a trip around the world, studying social and industrial conditions. At eighty-eight, she made a trip to South America, and, in order to be prepared for the trip, learned both Spanish and typewriting. At eighty-nine, she was a consulting psychologist in her own firm in San Francisco and, with four other senior citizens, was running a sixty-acre farm for profit in Marin County.

You see, the world may count you out, but God doesn't. Don't fail to take your last strike. Don't walk off the field in the ninth inning with two outs!

Anyone who knows sports will never forget the 1920 World Series between the Philadelphia Athletics and Chicago Cubs. Chicago won the first three games and was beating Philadelphia 8-0 when it went into the ninth inning. Philadelphia scored ten runs in the ninth inning and won the game. In the last game of that World Series, it was 3-2 Chicago with two outs in the ninth inning. But suddenly the Philadelphia team rallied to win not only the game but also the World Series! Sports literature is filled with such "come-from-behind" illustrations.

What about those people of God with a flagging will to fulfill their divine restoration assignment? They needed someone to help them get back on the field and win *their* game. As they sat around observing a half-finished job that had become the mockery of the known world, God sent someone to say to them, "Get up — get at it! Who said you were on the sidelines? Who told you that what you're doing isn't important? Who told you there wasn't enough power and strength in you to do it?"

The word of the Lord came unto Zerubbabel, saying, "*...Not by might nor by power, but by My Spirit...*" (Zech. 4:6). *That word* is what will cause mountains to crumble. That word is what will complete the job, for in the lampstand God has given us there is a never-ending source of supply.

Folks have every right to walk their way into eternity, saved only by the skin of their teeth. And at the Judgment Seat of Christ, when the fire shall try their works to see what sort they are, they have every right to present to Him a foundation overlaid by grass, straw, stubble, and wood — one that will be consumed in a moment of fire. Every person has a right to be saved, as First Corinthians 3:15 (*KJV*) says, "so as by fire."

But what about you? If you one day approach the Judgment Seat of Christ in such a sad condition, it won't be because you weren't good enough, powerful enough, or called enough, but because you allowed the enemy of your soul to sidetrack you by failure, guilt, and condemnation. You used the excuse of age, weakness, and ten thousand other things to keep you from the job God has placed your name on.

Zerubbabel knew the truth of these words, as did Joshua the high priest. And whether you are male or female, you have a name that rings with the same authenticity of God's call that those two

173

men had. God says, "In your name and in your call is the sufficiency to do the job I've given you to do." If you're sidetracked — if you're kept from your divinely assigned task — it is your own fault; it is *never* God's.

You say, "But my garments are dirty. I'm defiled."

He'll strip you in a moment and clothe you with linen.

You say, "It's been so long since I've been filled with the Spirit. I'm as dry as last year's bird's nest."

Ask Him to fill you anew. In but a moment, He'll satisfy your spirit with the water of life, and the oil of the Spirit will flow into the lamp of your heart and burn like a beacon to this world.

My friend, if you're sidetracked today from that job God has given you to do, it's the enemy of your soul who has found a way to stop your progress. Denounce his work; turn away from the Sanballats and Tobiahs; and begin again to rebuild the wall or the temple God has given you to build. It's time to do what God has called you to do!

May I offer this prayer:

> Father, I pray for my fellow believer, for the burden of this message is overwhelming to me. Lord, I know a multitude of empty-handed Christians will one day stand in Your Presence, having stopped short of Your goal for their lives because of the enemy's lies. Perhaps they experienced failure or weakness; perhaps they made a wrong decision or had bad timing on a right decision.

> But I ask, oh God, that by Your Spirit You would stir us up. May we will rebuild the walls and the temple of our lives. Oh, Father, may we hear Thy voice and not the voice of our accuser. May we rise to build as one person.

Father, I pray for this reader, whose spirit may be wounded and bruised and who may have accepted the lie that age, past failures, resentment, or anything else can sideline a believer from a God-given task that has his or her name on it. May the wounds of this precious child of Yours be healed, Lord. May Your voice come to him or her more strongly than ever before, saying, "This is the word of God unto you — not by might, nor by power, but by My Spirit shall this mountain be moved!"

Oh, Father, I pray that You will give us supernatural ability to know the enemy's rationalizations that come to our minds like devilish birds, picking the seed of the Word out of the freshly turned soil of our lives. Father, in the Name of Jesus we bind the enemy. We pray that his works and his lies shall be destroyed and that the captives shall be set free in Jesus' Name. May we be liberated to be Your sons and daughters and to go forth in the power and anointing of Your Name to fulfill Your purposes."

Now may Your benediction rest upon this dear reader, Father, in the Name of Your Son, Jesus Christ, and in the communion and fellowship of the Holy Spirit. Amen.

# SUMMARY

Satan could never change God's mind about you! The enemy can't cause you to backslide or send you to hell. When hell is eventually opened for business, Satan will be its victim, not its landlord.

What then can the devil do? Why is he so successful against Christians? He brings us into condemnation — a territory never entered by the Lord. Through accusation and blame, the enemy tries to cause us to detour from God's purposes in our lives.

In this arena, our enemy often wins the battle without firing a shot. The believer stands, head bowed under a burden of guilt, unable or unwilling to hear the Lord and totally debilitated from fulfilling his God-assigned mission.

Restoration is always on the heart of God. It is His purpose to see anything or anyone belonging to His covenant come into the *fullness* of His divine intention. He calls us always to restore our lives, our families, our churches, and our societies to their fullest and highest realization. There is no higher calling.

Of course, to determine to embark on restoration is to alert every enemy of God's intentions and to bring down on our heads demonic strategies aimed at stopping our progress. But greater indeed is the power within us than that of our enemy (1 John 4:4)!

Thus, hearing God's summons must be followed by a constant willingness to hear God's solutions. Restorers themselves must stay restored.

# APPENDIX

# STUDY QUESTIONS BY CHAPTER

## CHAPTER 1

Have you had an experience with God where you thought He was leading in one direction, only to find out later that He was leading you to a totally different ultimate purpose? If so, discuss it. Was the "ultimate" direction to a greater end?

## CHAPTER 2

Can you name and describe a restoration project in your home area? Was there local opposition to the project? What do you think of the outcome?

Has God called you to restore areas of your own life? Your family? Your local church? The community in which you live or society in general? Describe and discuss.

Do you believe God has an ultimate concern about a direction you are pursuing? Is there a sense of a "God Contract" — a divine assignment — for your church, project, or family? Describe.

## CHAPTER 3

Can you think of a childhood experience similar to the author's "KALAMAZOO" experience that has had a continuing effect on your life? Tell the story. What is the continuing effect?

## CHAPTER 4

The rebuilding of the temple in the destroyed Jerusalem was a "raison d'etre" for the returning Jews. Can you describe a similar central cause or issue that would easily mark a clear restoration in your community or family? Would it be a rebuilt spiritual center? Would it include restoration of relationships? What would it look like?

Have you read or heard of Haggai before? Was there an impact from his prophecy on you? Describe.

## CHAPTER 5

Tell about a time when God had to get your attention through a difficult experience. How long was it before you recognized His hand in your circumstances? Explain.

## CHAPTER 6

Can you tell about a remodeling project you undertook? Was it anything like "The Money Trap" mentioned in Chapter 2? Did you identify with Jim Williams' quote from his college professor about how to avoid being defeated in remodeling?

Have you seen *secular* sources or people used to correct God's people (e.g., Cyrus and the restoration of God's temple)? Explain what you discovered.

Do you identify with external and internal opposition to God's purposes? Could you illustrate this?

Have there been unique moments when you were refreshed to know "God remembers"? Could you describe one such time?

The "word of God" often overtakes generations, as it did Haggai's generation with the divine call to rebuild the temple. Can you give an illustration of this in our modern day?

## CHAPTER 7

Discuss a time in your life when to obey the will of God meant releasing a treasured relationship or moving from a protected place.

## CHAPTER 8

Haggai's insistence that God's people were acting on a false belief that "the time had not come" to rebuild the temple is *convicting*. Have you ever been in circumstances where you or others resisted fulfilling God's purpose by such reasoning? Describe.

The house of God — both the tabernacle and temple — was always central to the people of Israel. What project, purpose, or building do you see as central to God's people today?

Do you have a clear list of personal priorities? Name them.

Does Haggai's warning, "Consider your ways, for you sow and bring in little; eat but don't have enough," make sense to you? How would you apply it to today?

## CHAPTER 9

Relate a time in your life when God used a redirection of your plans to bring your life to a deeper spiritual purpose.

## CHAPTER 10

Have you ever participated in a true revival as told in Haggai 1:12-15 — a time when the Word of God brought repentance and change? Tell others about it. Describe its effects. Was there a specific response to that revival, as there was when Haggai told the people, "Go up to the mountains and get stones for building" (*see* Chapter 8)? What was the outcome?

How do you believe a "stirred-up spirit" is practically demonstrated in a person's life?

## CHAPTER 11

Have you had a church experience in which leadership was "turned negatively," such as Rick Howard describes? What happened? Was it ever resolved, or are its negative fruits still in evidence?

## CHAPTER 12

Are there times when you wonder if God's real focus is on His people? Describe such an experience.

Is God really a God of the valleys (*see* 1 Kings 20:28)?

Is it hard to believe that common men ultimately beat under the "horns" of authority? Can you name any recent experiences where this has occurred?

## CHAPTER 13

What did you learn when you first read about the loss of the Ark of God to the Philistines? Does superstition replace reality in many Christians' and Jews' experience today?

What does "coming out of Babylon" mean to you? Are you aware that there are seven biblical calls to "come out of Babylon"? Discuss the application of this to contemporary life.

Is it possible for believers to still lose money and possessions in a modern Babylon when their money and possessions are destined for use in the Kingdom of God? Reread the story in Chapter 13 about Willard Cantelon and the woman who offered her life savings to his ministry after World War II. Discuss.

## CHAPTER 14

Describe your first experience with young love.

Can you be open enough to describe your basic self-attitudes between the ages of 12 and 16? What experience in that period of time has affected your life?

## CHAPTER 15

Zerubbabel and Joshua needed to know that their very life purpose was associated with a task God gave them to do. Is that true of you?

Read Zechariah 4 aloud. What does verse 6 mean to you in its actual context, rather than simply as it is frequently quoted? Describe.

## CHAPTER 16

Do you know what "red-shirted" means as used in sports? What can cause it?

Are you able to candidly discuss an incident or experience that sidelined you from God's purpose? What happened?

## CHAPTER 17

Have you had an experience like Rick Howard — returning to a physical place that had a special place in your personal history? What happened to you?

Do you have a physical or emotional handicap? How has it affected your perception of life? Of God? Of others?

## CHAPTER 18

Are you aware of a failure in your life that Satan has used to bring condemnation? Are you free to discuss this? How did you prevent this from stopping progress in your Christian experience?

Have you ever felt like Joshua in Zechariah's fourth vision (*see* Zechariah 3)?

## CHAPTER 19

Do you understand the principle of representation? What role does it play in intercession?

Have you ever read Derek Prince's book, *Shaping History through Prayer and Fasting*? Do you believe modern-day Christians are God's agents for change? Are the ones you know acting as such? Discuss.

What does God's description of Christians as "kings and priests" mean to you on a practical level?

## CHAPTER 20

Rick answered the board in that critical meeting, "I told you I couldn't be voted into this church — God would have to send me. Well, I know it is God's will for me to bring my family here and pastor this church, and I can't be frightened out of that fact now."

What did you perceive from that response? Have you ever had a similar experience where neither circumstance nor human acceptance could determine God's purpose for you? What did *you* do?

## CHAPTER 21

What does it mean to you that God intends to rule from Zion (Ps. 110:2)?

Are you aware of how "monotonous drivel" can become an apt description of church focus? Can you explain this?

Do Christians fall short of God's purpose by accepting lesser purposes? How?

Do you know the words to the chorus, "Keep Me True, Lord Jesus"? Can you sing it? Do you often think of the significance of staying "on course"?

## CHAPTER 22

What do you think Jesus was referring to when He talked about "counting the cost to finish the building"? Can you relate that to current experiences?

What do you believe actually stops progress in fulfilling God's purposes? Can you name specific examples?

Rick Howard writes, "...Joshua the high priest can't in any way effectively intercede and mediate on behalf of God while he is in a place of accusation." Has this experience ever been true in your life? Describe.

## CHAPTER 23

Reread Rick Howard's experience with his handicap. Have you ever had feelings like he describes?

Did the Holy Spirit bring you to a specific answer concerning your inadequacies and God's purposes? Tell how.

## CHAPTER 24

Please review the C. S. Lewis quote in this chapter. How does Satan neutralize the effectiveness of Christians?

How would you explain personally Ruth Paxton's idea of despoiling, decoying, and disabling Christians? Give personal examples.

How have you witnessed Satan's use of these "widespread" feelings of inadequacy and inferiority in detouring Christians from God's purpose for their lives?

What do you believe is the answer to this problem?

## CHAPTER 25

Dr. Dobson's examples of deep feelings of inferiority as quoted by one author touch many of us. Do you feel that such feelings of inferiority have affected your life? If so, how? If not, why not?

Do you relate to the Eleanor Rigby experience? Could it happen in your church?

## CHAPTER 26

Our author describes a time when he faced the Joshua experience by asking God, "Why did you wait sixteen years to tell Joshua this?" Do you remember God's answer? Does that strike a chord in you as you consider your own walk with God? Is there something God has been trying to tell you that you have been unable or unwilling to receive?

## CHAPTER 27

Could you retell the experience of Zechariah jumping into his own vision?

Do you understand or relate to the need for people to help other people with self-esteem? Illustrate.

When Rick Howard cried out, "Oh, how I long for such a friend," and he heard God answer, "Become such a friend," what do you believe was the deeper message?

Do you relate to the principle of changing what you can before God changes what you can't? Describe an example from your own life.

## CHAPTER 28

Can you illustrate from your own life experience people who were sidetracked by age or by other obstacles, but who then went on to accomplish great purposes? Name them. What changed their experience from one of defeat to one of victory?

How about you? How does *Restoring Restorers* apply to you? To others in your life?

# OTHER BOOKS
# BY RICK C. HOWARD

*Songs From Life* (hardback)

*Strategy for Triumph: A Christian Perspective on Problems*

*The Finding Times of God*

*The Judgment Seat of Christ*

*The Judgment Seat of Christ* (Spanish)

*The Lost Formula of the Early Church* (hardback)

*Seven Biblical Steps to Personal Renewal*

*This Was Your Life* (co-authored with Jamie Lash)

# ABOUT THE AUTHOR

Rick C. Howard is a pastor whose pulpit is the world. He is the author of thirteen books, including the best-selling *The Judgment Seat of Christ*, now translated in Chinese, Spanish, and Bulgarian. Two of his books are translated in more than thirty languages.

Rick is a frequent speaker at conferences and has ministered in more than seventy-five nations. He served on the faculty of a major Christian college for fourteen years and is presently adjunct faculty of Asia Pacific Theological Seminary. Rick's pastorate in the San Francisco Bay area lasted thirty years. He is currently the Apostolic/Missions Pastor of the same church and remains committed to the message of restoration and reconciliation.

# Naioth Sound and Publishing

2995 Woodside Road, Suite 400
Toll free: 1-800-726-3127
Fax: 1-650-368-0790


Discounts for volume amounts:
40% discount for bookstores
50% discount for churches
60% discount for distributors